Beneath the Ancient Dust

Beneath the Ancient Dust

Inspirational Stories
From Nine Years in Afghanistan

Melissa R. Meyers

2018

ISBN 978-0-692-08707-7

Edited by Connie Anderson, Words and Deeds, Inc.
Interior and Cover Design by Sue Stein

Cover photo © Melissa R. Meyers
Author photo © Marit-Williams Photography

To John, Malcolm, and Emily who journeyed with me—
and to the people of Afghanistan, may one day
your beautiful country have peace.

Disclosure

Due to the sensitive nature of working in Afghanistan, all the names in the book have been changed, except mine, my family's names, those I have permission to use, and the names that I consider public knowledge due to media coverage. Most of the events on the journey of the Salang Pass occurred on the first journey like described, but I traveled it many times in those early days. So it became difficult to remember what details I saw that first journey compared to the multiple journeys so details like seeing the tents selling honey and villages clinging to mountainsides were condensed into one. Some areas, places, names, and details where events took place have been changed to protect Afghan friends and co-workers' identities, since even working for foreign agencies can be dangerous for them and their families. The conversations and the events have not been changed.

Table of Contents

Timeline

John and I visit Afghanistan for a two-week trip—summer of 2004
Malcolm is born in America—June 2005
Move to Kabul, Afghanistan for six months—October 2005
Move to Mazar-e-Sharif in northern Afghanistan—April 2006
Emily is born—July 2008
Move to Faizabad in northeastern Afghanistan—May 2009
Move back to Kabul, Afghanistan—August 2013
Move back to Minnesota—May 2014

Introduction

"That's it! We can't fit one more thing in here. Melissa, do you think we can buy sheets when we arrive?"

"I don't see why not. Take them out, John." Famous last words.

Why and how do you pack up your family and move overseas? How do you do this when you are moving to a landlocked country that has been at war for the past thirty years—and has no working postal service, no ground shipping, and we can't even send a shipping carton?

First, you have a gigantic garage sale, and sell almost everything. What's left still ends up being way too much stuff to fit into large-sized gray totes that could weigh up to 70 pounds each; three total, one for my husband, the baby, and me. The fourteen-pound baby needed as much stuff as his parents.

Now in the fall of 2005, as we checked in our three totes and juggled our extremely over-weight hand luggage, baby stroller and carry-ons through airport security, it wasn't "my stuff" I was afraid to leave behind. I was sad to leave the kitchen table and the Ansell Adams prints, but it was our parents, siblings, aunts, uncles, grandmas, grandpas, friends, and church family I wanted to pack up and move overseas with me. In a matter of moments, my whole support network was left on the runway of the Minneapolis airport.

Not being accustomed to traveling with a small baby, it was hectic going through security, but once I had boarded the airplane, I had a quiet moment to think about our journey and how we got to this point.

For John and me, it started with an infamous day in U.S. history that marked many other people's lives. In 2001, we were seniors at a Bible college in Minnesota. As part of our college's study-abroad program, we both had spent nine months of our junior year in other countries. I in Kenya, and John in a place called Peshawar, Pakistan. John had spent nine months teaching high school and university students English. Many of them were Afghan refugees who had fled to Pakistan due to the unrest and the atrocious government that was in power, the Taliban.

For us September 11, 2001 started like any other day. John and I were in a college classroom when suddenly a person interrupted the class to let us know something terrible was happening. A feeling of confusion was in the air, and several students started to get up. The instructor, not under-standing the totality of what occurred, told us to sit down so he could finish class. Everyone left class when the television in a nearby lounge was turned on. In horror we watched replays of an airplane crashing into one of the twin towers. Not long afterwards we watched as another airplane smashed into the side of the adjacent tower. Then both towers collapsed.

Later, stories about the horrors of what had been happening in Afghanistan under the Taliban government began to emerge. Perhaps, the stories had been there all the time, but John and I, like many others, listened for the first time. My heart was stirred, and I prayed a simple prayer, "Lord, use me there." Our senior year continued. We had previously become engaged in August 2001, and we planned on getting married after graduation in the summer of 2002. Both of us graduated with degrees in Cross-cultural Communication and Missions. We had always planned on working some-place overseas. After getting married, we moved to Rochester, Minnesota, where I enrolled in a two-year nursing course, so we had a little time to figure things out.

At first, not wanting to commit to working in an extreme place like Afghanistan, we explored other places. Through a long time of prayer and inquiry, we decided on exploring moving to Afghanistan late in 2003. John desired to do this because of his work with Afghan refugees in Pakistan, and I did because the stories about how Afghan women had suffered touched me deeply.

In the summer of 2004, after I graduated with my RN degree, we took a two-week trip to visit a family that John had lived with in Pakistan, and who had since moved to Kabul. During our ten days there, we connected with a Christian international aid and development organization through which John could work as an English teacher and I as a nurse. We returned to Minnesota. I started working as a Registered Nurse, and John became certified as a teacher of English as a Second Language, and raised support for the volunteer organization we would work with.

Then, we became pregnant with our first child. Having visited Afghanistan in the summer, I knew many international families already lived there. It would be challenging, but we could still go. In June of 2005, Malcolm was born. Almost four months later, we packed up our belongings ready to make the biggest move of our lives.

We spent the first six months in the capital city of Kabul, learning one of the languages spoken in Afghanistan, Dari, a Persian dialect. Then the organization we joined wanted us to move north to the city of Mazar-e-Sharif where they had an English language institute. After Malcolm was a little older, I planned on working as a nurse part-time.

That morning in October 2005, I felt like I was carried away in a whirlwind, and before I could even catch my breath, we had boarded our plane in Minneapolis. In what felt like a short time, we landed on a runway in New Delhi for a ten-hour layover, in a completely foreign place. The next ten hours were spent with my four-month-old baby in a lounge with dim lighting, dirty couches, and a big, grizzly bartender. This should have indicated to me that many things were going to change in the near future.

Finally, we boarded our destination flight to Afghanistan.

Three hours later, we landed on the dusty runway leading to the international airport of Kabul. Deep breaths went through me as we descended the stairs leading to the airstrip below. The full sunlight hit us that autumn day as we waited for a bus to come and take us to the airport buildings. Military vehicles and choppers could be seen on various parts of the runway, reminding me of the ongoing conflict that the National Atlantic Treaty Organization (NATO) alliance, along with the Afghan nation, was in with the Taliban.

As we waited patiently, a young Afghan woman approached us; her eyelashes thick with mascara, and her headscarf perched loosely on her jet-black hair. Smiling, she pinched Malcolm's cheek. "What a little doll!" she said in perfect English. We would discover most of the Afghan people were bystanders in the current conflict. Their daily lives interrupted by explosions, suicide bombers, and military patrols. Some were seeing their home country for the first time ever, because they were born overseas from immigrant parents. They came to see a land they knew only through stories and another's eyes.

Finally, a gigantic beat-up white-and-blue bus came and we boarded it, and swayed toward the customs building. After making it through the long lines of people entering the country, our passports were stamped with approval, and we stood around the chaotic baggage claim waiting for our three plastic totes to arrive via the luggage belt. The ancient-looking belt churned into motion as we anxiously awaited our meager possessions.

Fortunately all the totes arrived. In those days there were no carts lined up for travelers to use. Porters aggressively forced rickety luggage carts toward you. Our luggage was grabbed and loaded, whether we liked it or not, and we slowly exited the airport, walking behind the man whose cart carrying all our possessions lurched erratically left and right.

A woman, who later would become one of my closest friends, approached us carrying a baby girl in her arms. In a European accent, she asked, "Are you the Meyers?"

"Yes!" We were happy to have anyone identify us.

"I am Mirjam. I will take you to the car." I looked at her baby, maybe ten months, streaked with dirt that she picked up from the airport floor during their long wait. The fine dust seemed to permeate every crevice and chink. I glanced down at Malcolm, wondrously clean, and I groaned thinking, *Is this how my baby is going to look living here in this dirt-covered county?* As we approached the car, Mirjam saw our three totes and warily said, "You have brought a lot of stuff!"

I thought of all we had left behind, and how all we owned had been reduced to these three totes, and I wondered: *haven't I given up enough?* Little did I know of the challenges we would face. I was naïve about how much I would have to adapt my everyday life to live in Afghan culture, especially an extremely conservative Muslim culture. Yet, little did I realize how much I would gain, and how many changes lay ahead.

We lived in Afghanistan for almost nine years. Moved four different times: Kabul, Mazar-e-Sharif, Faizabad, then back to Kabul again. In the year 2008, I flew home to America to give birth to our daughter Emily.

John worked as an English teacher for three years, a Regional Manager in Faizabad for four years, where we had a community development project, hydro-power project, and adult learning education project. When we moved to Kabul, he moved into the role of Director of Regional Managers that supported the seven different regions in Afghanistan where projects were in operation. I had various part-time jobs during my years in Afghanistan. I worked in a government-run hospital supporting their nursing school, helped direct and teach at a bilingual preschool for four years when my children were little, worked with Birth and Life Saving Skills (BLiSS), which was a community development group for women to learn about safe birth practices, and in Kabul, I worked at an eye hospital.

Over those years, I heard a multitude of stories, learned spiritual lessons, and I started to write. In the end, I hope I was a blessing to the Afghan people in many ways—as I feel the Afghan people greatly blessed me.

Chapter 1

Traveling the Treacherous and Breathtaking Salang Pass to Mazar-e-Sharif

An Invitation to Go on a Journey

In the pre-dawn hours, Kabul was a silent, slumbering giant. For the past six months, I had lived in this notorious city located in eastern Afghanistan, navigating its jarring side streets that gave way to freshly paved roads. During the day, I walked these streets where commuters pedaled their 1950's-style bicycles. On the same street, trucks carried adolescent soldiers toting AK-47s, while overburdened donkeys, fruit-sellers, and uniformed school children co-existed with women who were wearing smartly cut suits while bedecked in ornate headscarves and three-inch stilettos. I would soon realize that travel across the city was easy—when the people of Kabul were all safely tucked away in their beds.

That morning, my husband, John, and our nine-month-old son, Malcolm, and I were about to travel via the Salang highway to our new home in the northern city of Mazar-e-Sharif. We had finished a six-month language school in Kabul and were moving north so John could begin his job as a teacher of English as a Second Language. I later hoped to be able to work or volunteer as a nurse.

In the midst of changing our blond-haired and blue-eyed son's diaper with a flashlight clutched between my teeth, a horn honked. Several other expatriates—people from all over the world who would be traveling with us that day—were all waiting when the passenger van, a *tunis*, finally arrived.

I turned and shut the white wooden door of the home we had occupied during a phase in our lives when we completed intensive language study and had started new jobs with an international aid organization. I glanced at John, our eyes locked for a moment, affirming the mutual understanding of our commitment to go ahead. Then together the three of us went through the gate into the muddy street and climbed into the vehicle. We greeted the other travelers, three adults and their two early-elementary-aged children. After saying a prayer together for safe travels, the driver nodded to my husband, and the door slid shut.

During this late fall of 2005, the nation still pulsated with hope. Buildings, roads, ancient ruins, and businesses were repaired at an industrious rate, and in those days, the nation enjoyed a time of fragile peace. The eight-to-nine hour trip we embarked on via the Salang highway that day wouldn't have been possible several years earlier. The Northern Alliance, an anti-Taliban resistance group, while fighting the Taliban, blew the tunnel entrance shut, hoping to stall the tide of the Taliban washing over the land.

In the last few years with the joint effort of several countries, the historic road had reopened, the tunnel unearthed, and with this gesture, the long-abandoned trade route flourished again. Storekeepers and restaurant owners dusted off their locked doors and reopened a world that has always been part of Afghanistan—one of trade and commerce operating since the days of the ancient Silk Road.

As of that morning, I had not yet discovered these things. My time in Kabul had given me a taste of Afghanistan, but during my travels I really began to experience its heart and its history—albeit a broken one.

Besides the Taliban, its most recent invaders were the Soviet Union in 1979, and not surprisingly I kept stumbling upon the imprint that they left all over the country. As the driver flew through the city, we passed a dilapidated mustard-yellow Soviet wheat silo and bread factory; its current function was to simply testify about a former occupation, and to act as a landmark for directions.

Seeing how this monstrosity loomed in the middle of the city, I thought of the humble mud *tandoors*, where Afghans baked their bread. In contrast, I discovered these yellow fading silos dotted the landscape in almost every predominant city along the Salang Pass. I would come to learn that the Russians in an early partnership with Afghanistan in the 1960s first helped the Afghan nation build its infrastructure.[1] The bread factories were built to feed their workers, which later fed the Russian army's stomach when it invaded Afghanistan. The Russian's audacity and advance planning struck me that morning as we passed it. Then the whipping wind blew the trees, and I imagined this relic of a former era someday eroding away.

Sometimes my life feels as if some unknown force is blowing the seconds, minutes, and days quickly by, and like water flowing through my fingers, it cannot be grasped or grabbed or held onto.

Looking back, the outer limits of Kabul disappeared, and the *tunis* jerked as we began our ascent. At the next corner, we saw a gushing snow-fed mountain stream. The van chugged up a steep hillside, and veered to the right. Our driver, a broad-shouldered, somber man, hit the brakes, commanding the vehicle to an abrupt stop.

Hundreds of sheep and goats spanned the narrow road. As the animals engulfed the tunis, a tiny old woman, wearing brilliant green and blue clothing, seized an enormous black ram by its gnarled horns and stubbornly directed him out of the flow of traffic, laughing the whole time. Her face was full of wrinkles caused by the unyielding elements of the earth. Seeing these nomadic peoples traveling with their flocks of sheep and goats made me begin to question what century this was because these encounters transported me back to an ancient land—and a certain book.

Part of why I was on this journey was because as a teenager, I found a message of love in an ancient text. Within the historic pages of the Bible, I had read about similar images and nomadic tribes. But, it wasn't until I set foot on Afghan soil that I encountered them in the flesh. As we passed the sheep and the goats moving into the surrounding hills to feast on the spring grasses, the scriptures became alive, and I began to connect it to my own life in a way like never before.

Throughout the scriptures, a multitude of stories tell about people moving. For the past year, my family and I had been on this huge transition of coming from America to settle in a foreign country. With trepidation and resolve, my husband and I gave up our jobs, boarded an airplane with Malcolm, and moved to a war-torn nation. Now, when I finally felt like I was beginning to find my way, we were journeying again.

The laughing woman and her animals passed, and we continued to ascend the winding mountain road. Small villages made up of rock and mud clinging to mountainsides where people have dwelled for centuries popped into view. There, as the sun crested over the horizon, I glimpsed a family. They sat on top of their flat mud-roof house with a mountain stream roaring underneath. Piles of cotton surrounded them, and the father, mother, and several children meticulously fluffed it up and pushed it back into the long mattress casings used in every Afghan home. Farther down the road, crude signs appeared that read, "Honey," and ten-year-old shopkeepers waved sporadically as the vehicles chugged on by. Their makeshift stores housed jar upon jar of the sweet nectar.

Around nine, we pulled over to a wayside restaurant to have breakfast. As we stepped out of the vehicle, we were amazed. The jagged mountains rose above us, like a gigantic cathedral designed by God, battered by the wear and tear of Mother Nature and Father Time. The waiter, in his early teens, came to take our orders. New to Afghan traveling cuisine, we were surprised to find the menu choices were limited to kabobs, naan (the traditional flat bread), tea, and sodas. After the twists and turns on the road, meat was the last thing we wanted. A pot of tea and some bread were ordered. Piping hot green tea was poured into glass cups from a copper kettle, refreshing our little traveling group as we sat on the floor around a plastic tablecloth. One of our traveling companions pulled out a small round cake he'd purchased from a Kabul bakery, and we feasted on cardamom-flavored cake, along with the bread and tea, while seated in the cool mountain air. Despite the beauty all around us, I continued to wonder about the changes ahead.

After enjoying the refreshing tea, we scouted out a bathroom, which was nothing more than a mud brick outhouse, the doorway covered with a ragged sheet. Then back in the van, we continued our ascent. Gradually, the tunis slowed because of traffic congestion as we neared the entrance of the Salang Tunnel where we saw the remains of an old work site covered with a dusting of snow. Forty years prior, they housed Russian workers, many of them boys on the brink of adulthood. These adolescent boys had achieved the monstrous feat of digging through sheer granite, precisely at 11,034 feet in elevation, but with the crisp air and cold winds, it must have felt like the top of the world.

Finally, it was our vehicle's turn, and we entered the roughly mile-and-a-half long tunnel void of any electric lights. In the beginning, shafts of light streamed in every couple of feet through cracks and crevices in the tunnel wall. Old broken gas pipes ran along the inside of the tunnel. The road was worn away in spots, causing our driver to maneuver around a lot of potholes. The exhaust was thick, and although all our windows were rolled up tight, it seeped in. The passengers in the car fell silent.

The darkness engulfed our traveling entourage as we arrived at the heart of the tunnel, submerged in stone, high above thousands of feet of earth. The air was stifling, and the headlights of the vehicle dim. For a second, I worried about the van having a flat tire in the middle of this beast, but then shook the terrible thought away. Creeping forward, at last, a far-off light appeared. Abruptly, a gigantic *camaiz* barreled down on the *tunis*, and our driver, clenching the wheel, lurched the van to the side as the truck roared past, leaving us shaking in our smallness.

The dim light grew into a blaze, and we burst forth free from the belly of the stone creature. The windows were cracked open, and in flowed the crisp, fresh air. Malcolm stirred, blinked, and I reached for his hand to assure him I was still there. The *tunis* turned a corner onto a road that cascaded down the mountainside. It was dangerously narrow at parts, without any side rails to prevent us from careening off the cliff.

The swaying motion continued, and I dozed for what must have been several hours. Upon awakening, I realized that the road had flattened out. All the snow and greenery had gone. Several camels in the distance regally traversed their own path. Was it perhaps a mirage from the days of the Old Silk Road? The dust rose, and I wondered what the city of Mazar would be like. After passing through a narrow gorge of rock, a lush city emerged where the snowy blossoms of the apricot trees bloomed.

"Is this Mazar?" I asked the driver, growing hopeful because it was so lovely.

"No, it's Tash-kur-ghan, a village near Mazar."

A river ran through the village, and the contrast struck me—land with life-giving water was also a land void of this precious commodity. Shortly, we reentered the desert, and the van began to coast. I suddenly sat up straight, realizing the driver wasn't doing it to save gas, the tunis had broken down.

Miles from Kabul, with only rudimentary language skills, John and I were the only ones in the vehicle who could communicate with the driver. The driver, his dark eyes exhausted and weary, demanded his fee for the day, proceeded to empty our belongings from the vehicle, and explained this was as far as he could take us. A few small shops lined the road near our broken-down vehicle. Soon words were exchanged between the driver and John, and also some of the shopkeepers. I stood helplessly by with the others in our traveling group, bouncing Malcolm up and down on my hip, and straining to hear and make out the few phrases I understood, trying to grasp what would become of us.

John explained in his broken Dari about the urgency for us to arrive in Mazar before sunset. An hour later, five adults (not counting the driver), the two small children, Malcolm, and way too much luggage, crammed into a hatchback taxi. It was now after midday, and a sweltering sun had replaced the lovely spring weather. So we would all fit into the taxi, being five-feet-tall and the size of a young teen, I was elected to sit up front on the lap of the one of the other woman traveling with us.

Now Malcolm was stuck in the back without me, and after only a couple miles down the road, began to scream. John tried to offer him a cookie, anything to keep him quiet. "John, where's his pacifier?" I asked, awkwardly turning my head to see his face.

John said, "In the back of the taxi in the diaper bag." With all the commotion we hadn't planned well. We needed to stop, so I pleaded with our new driver who was hunched over the wheel, probably wondering how he had gotten himself into such a mess with this strange group of foreigners and their wailing baby.

When he pulled over to the side of the road, I quickly got out, opened the back of the vehicle, grabbed Malcolm's pacifier and favorite blanket and thrust them at John, hoping it would help. It didn't.

An hour later, the city of Mazar came into view. A dust storm had started, and dirt and grit swirled around our vehicle. Glancing out the window, all I could make out was drab mud walls. The temperature had risen to over ninety, and sweat poured down my face—and everyone else's in the taxi.

My heart sank…of all the beautiful places we had passed that day, we seemed to have come to the most desolate spot.

"What have I done?" I whispered. "God, where have you taken me?"

Had you known me as a child, Afghanistan was the last place you would have expected me to end up. But, life can be like that. Sometimes, it leads us to the unexpected places, and in this case, it led me into the heart of a proud nation struggling to throw off the beasts of poverty as well as a horrific world image.

As a teenager, I started to travel with Christian groups to developing countries that were extremely different from my sleepy Midwestern hometown of six hundred inhabitants, and in these travels I not only encountered beauty, but also extreme poverty, and I began to glimpse the heart of God for those in such situations.

For the first time, I encountered real pain caused by war, dictatorships, famine caused by land depletion, injustice of sexes, and personal tragedies. I wasn't just seeing them on the television, reading about them in magazines, or hearing about them on the radio. I couldn't change a channel or click off these images.

In these places I witnessed street children who were addicted to sniffing glue wiping the windshield of a taxi or selling sticks of gum for one and two cent coins. I visited orphanages where row after row of iron beds housed rejected children who were wailing for someone to come and love them, or worse, they stared blankly into space, having accepted the reality that no one ever would. Women in torn and dirty clothes, clutching babies pacified with opium to quiet their cries of hunger, pulled on my arms and the back of my coat, pressing me for a bit of cash. And, my perception of the world that had been based on my Midwestern upbringing, now shattered like glass.

In contrast with the heartrending injustices of the world, in my other travels, I also encountered the salty blue-green ocean, the plains of Africa alive with exotic creatures, carpeted mountains, rainbow-encircled waterfalls, and flamingo-filled lakes. I witnessed children playing in ghettos whose laughter splashed and somersaulted over the open sewers and past the garbage heaps.

All those experiences had led me to a dry and dusty city in northern Afghanistan, wanting to make a difference, but wondering where God was in all of this. Had I known the end, I might have urged the original driver to turn around, and sped down the mountain until I reached the runway of the Kabul Airport. But leaving Afghanistan was nine years in the future, nine years of daily life unfolding, nine years of discovering the truths of God in this wild land, and nine years of joy intermingled with extreme heartbreak. I would have missed out on the whispers of God through the drug smugglers, taxi-driving shepherds, a beggar girl called Bahar, a Buddhist monastery, treacherous road journeys, encounters with warlords, keeping chickens, the struggles of modern Afghan women, a foreign cemetery, and Afghan weddings.

I didn't know the end, and that's the beauty of a journey. Journeying takes us outside of our everyday lives, and awakens our souls.

Chapter 2

Protective Walls of Rubble and Stone

Allowing God to Touch Our Pain

My adventurous journey of scaling the mountain road of the Salang highway turned into a monotonous plod shortly after moving to Mazar-e-Sharif.
Every morning I entered the kitchen, and sat down at a little white table we
had scrounged up somewhere. As I would sip my morning cup of coffee,
make small talk about the day with John as he munched on cornflakes
and mixed-up powdered milk, I would feed Malcolm his bowl of mushy
oatmeal. Staring out the large three-panel kitchen window, my eyes fixated
on the fourteen-foot-high mud walls around our home. I was going
through full-blown culture shock. The compound was small, and in the
early morning summer heat, I glowered at the drab walls that I wished
would fall like those famous walls of Jericho.

The walls in Afghan society were negative reminders of division, of the
constant separation maintained between unrelated men and women, and
of my own loss of freedom. Walls are an extensive part of every city and
most villages in this part of the world. When you walk down a street in
Afghanistan, it is not the houses that you first notice, but the walls, gates,
and doors that block out the private lives of the families dwelling in these
compounds.

Every house in a city is either in the middle of a walled-in area or the house is built as one side of the wall and the rest of the walls create an open courtyard. Afghan women use the courtyard area for washing dishes, doing laundry, planting small gardens, sometimes keeping chickens or goats, and usually there is an outside kitchen where they cook. All the houses that we lived in were designed this way. A metal or wooden door was the only access to life outside the courtyard.

* * *

Years later on a Saturday morning we would experience what happens when the boundaries of the walls are disrespected.

Mattie, our black-and-white mutt, growled and barked. Her barking was incessant, and our quiet weekend morning ceased to be restful. It had to stop. A little boy had been throwing rocks and sticks at our dog for the past half hour. Our verbal pleas to stop resulted in him sneaking around the corner of the next-door neighbor's roof, where he waited until we went back inside, and then continued his assault on our dog. This is when John got the ladder out and decided to physically shoo him off the roof, back to his home. It worked. The boy took off running.

John, though, made one disastrous error. He forgot the customary phrase he was supposed to call out as he was going up to let our neighbors, particularly the women, know that a man was climbing up the wall of the roof that bordered their property. This phrase served as a warning for the women to clear the courtyard so an unrelated man wouldn't see them. Afghan women cook, do laundry, and take naps out in their courtyards. Yelling out shows respect for them, but since we didn't grow up in this type of culture, it easily was forgotten. Moments, later we heard an angry pounding again and again on our metal gate. John tenuously opened the gate thinking it was perhaps the father of the boy he had scared away.

It wasn't. It was the eldest brother from next door. With his fists waving in the air, he spewed out profane words about John dishonoring the women of his household. Moments later, several women rushed out and threw themselves in front of their eldest brother, pleading with him to not do anything drastic.

John apologized and then decided the best course of action would be to slip away before a crowd began to gather. What followed was a heated discussion in the kitchen, where I chided John and this extreme culture for wrecking a perfectly good weekend. For the sake of preserving relationships with our direct neighbors, Angela, a co-worker who lived in an apartment downstairs from us, and I went bearing baklava and apologies. It appeared the women of their household had been offended, so we went as mediators to put it right.

The matriarch of the family came first, married since the age of fourteen, and not much older than me, her children ranged in age from two to twenty-two. The traditional greetings came first, accompanied by the three alternating kisses followed by a handshake. She was followed by her other daughters. Their slow grins and hasty greetings, which usually were so welcoming, puzzled me. I wondered whether they really were upset or slightly embarrassed at what had transpired. Angela and I were seated in the guest room, where we waited for the customary tea to be prepared, while we tried to explain what had happened. The women were gracious, and called their brother, *"daewana"* which means crazy, they accepted our baklava and our regrets.

It was a stern reminder of the walled society we lived in, the rules existing in Afghan society that are for the protection of women, and the extent that others are willing to enforce them when they are broken. It took me years to realize that the walls were not always negative.

In Afghanistan, the walls are built with several different materials. Historically, the walls were made out of flat stones and rocks hewn from the earth and interlaced in an incredibly complex pattern, and the cracks are filled up with mud. Another traditional way is to build them from mud bricks using an ancient technique still practiced today.

Our neighbors rebuilt a room on the top level of their home. I watched them tear the whole structure down, dirt flying and mud bricks disintegrating back into dust as they hit the pavement. As each brick came down, I could see into what remained of the interior of the room.

After the mess was cleared, a huge new pile of dirt appeared, along with sand and straw. They shaped a large circular trough, and water was piped into the dirt trough. Then the *gilkor*, a young man who wore a turban, a white muscle shirt, and had deep sun-tanned skin, took off his shoes. He hitched up his baggy pants and proceeded to slowly step into the oozing mud. With each step he methodically mixed in parts of straw, sand, and water.

Several hours later, he must have been pleased with the consistency of the mixture, for then he used a wooden mold, and he began to make the bricks. The mud was scooped into the four spaces, pressed down until no air pockets were left, then wiped smooth, and rapidly turned over. With great caution, the young man eased the mold off, and four perfect bricks were left to bake in the scorching sun. To build the walls for this room, he worked for several weeks, making hundreds of sunbaked bricks.

The *gilkor* built the walls of the room. Brick by brick he blocked out the sunshine, the stares of the neighbors, the sounds of the barking stray dogs, as well as the wedding music floating through the neighborhood. Building a wall like this takes an enormous amount of human power and time.

The ancient societies in Biblical times were walled civilizations. For example, in the book of Nehemiah, the Jewish nation finally returned to Jerusalem after the many years of sorrow and exile when they had been in captivity in Babylon.

> *Beside the waters of Babylon, there we sat down and wept,*
> *when we remembered Zion.*
> *On the willows there we hung up our lyres.*
> *For there our captors*
> *Required of us songs, and our tormentors, mirth, saying,*
> *"Sing us one of the songs of Zion!"*
> *How shall we sing the Lord's song in a foreign land?*
> —Psalm 137

The haunting Psalm depicted the broken-heartedness of the captive Israelites, who longed that their homeland would not be forgotten. In the book of Nehemiah, those who had been living in captivity had now begun to return to their beloved city. The long road trip is over, but the Jerusalem they remembered is no more. So the first thing they did was to begin to rebuild the walls.

When we first visited Afghanistan in the spring of 2004, much rubble and ruin was still visible, but Afghan citizens were flocking back to their country at a rapid speed, not unlike the displaced Israelites returning from Babylon, with a heart to take back what they had lost and what had been stolen. There was a great feeling of hope in the air, and a promise of a better future. Indeed, the Afghans who returned, along with those who had never left, were menders. They were menders of their cities, rebuilders of walls, and restorers of homes.

To me, as the homes and cities were restored, it was a symbol of healing as a nation.

The walls for the Israelite nation provided safety from their enemies, privacy for their families, and created structure and order to a city. The rebuilding of the walls in Afghanistan did the same.

I am not a stranger to walls for as a child I had built a thick wall around my own heart. I was a sensitive child, and when I was in third grade my father's alcoholism increased to a point where he went in for treatment. My family had deep wounds that needed to heal from my father's alcoholism, but it wasn't my family issues that caused me my greatest pain, and encouraged me to wall out those around me.

It was being a victim of bullying. When I turned eight, for first and second grade, I attended a small school in our town of six hundred. I had friends, and loved my teacher. The school district, like many schools in the 1980s, consolidated with the neighboring community. The next year, I boarded a bus, and headed six miles east. Six miles was all it took for my world to drastically change.

I was a shy child, and one of the first days, during recess or perhaps even at gym class, I was playing with some other children. One of them singled me out, asking, "Where are you from?"

"I'm from here," I replied.

"You can't be from here, listen to how you talk."

I didn't understand what he meant. "I'm from Minnesota; I've never lived anywhere else."

He then proceeded to mock me, and repeat my speech, ending with the words, "Freak."

From that day on, I endured a horrendous year of Drew mocking me every day. I dreaded seeing him or being anywhere near him. Most of all I didn't understand, for I had never done anything to him, nor had I ever experienced such hatred from another. I began to think something must really be wrong with me. I began to believe the things that he said about me. Since this was also the year my father's drinking problem escalated, I never told my parents what was going on.

In life, when pain comes our way, we can pack down all those little fragments of hurtful words and experiences into a wooden mold and pop out mud brick after mud brick that we stack around our hearts.

I got a lot of stomachaches that year, and remember the relief after I had told my mother I was too sick to go to school that day, when I hopped back into bed, opening up a book, and escaping into any world that wasn't mine.

For the month my father was in rehab, I am sure I didn't tell a soul.

I remember when my dad was finally going to come home. My mother gave me five dollars to go to the local grocery store and buy Dad a welcome-home gift. I thought five dollars was a lot of money, and that I probably could buy anything in the store. I looked at shelf after shelf, deciding what I could get him. I came across the aisle of snacks and nuts. I didn't want to buy him a bag of chips or peanuts. I wanted something special. And, there I saw it, a beautiful glass mug filled with peanuts, with the University of Minnesota's Gopher emblem on it. I was sure he would love it. It cost most of my five dollars. I brought it home, and my mother nearly flipped because I had bought a beer mug filled with peanuts. I hadn't known it was a beer mug. I so much wanted to get him something special.

The peanuts were dumped in a bowl. The mug disposed of somewhere, and that was my welcome home gift for my father. My heart was crushed, I was sure I couldn't do anything right.

I stacked mud brick upon mud brick to build my own wall.

As school continued, I learned how to stay out of Drew's way. My teacher picked up on the fact I had problems pronouncing my r's and s's so I was enrolled in speech therapy. The only problem was the speech therapist was also the special education teacher. I hated going because I so badly wanted to be "normal." I spent a lot of time using that word in my head, *normal.* "I am normal like everyone else," I often repeated to myself. If I could have built a physical wall, I would have at this point, but instead I retreated into myself and continued to emotionally wall out all those around me.

There are benefits to walls, but there are also dangers. In life, we can slowly erect walls—rocks, mud bricks, baked bricks, and concrete ones that we cement around our hearts. Sometimes, these are necessary walls, and because we are living in unbearable situations, we experience pain and hurt that unless we block it out, we feel we can't function. The walls get us through the hard times, and sometimes, they are able to protect us and keep us sane until we are in a place where we can process what has happened. As we fill up the chinks in the walls, add more and more bricks, something else can happen—the good gets walled out with the bad. Through the pain I experienced as a child, I built a wall around my heart that blocked out those around me.

As a child, pulling back and living in my own world helped me construct a sense of safety. Much like my Afghan neighbors who felt safe from prying eyes behind their walls—until one day when a stranger came climbing up on the roof unannounced. After John's accidental encounter with our neighbors, the friendship between their family and me continued to grow, so much that, to this day, I still have contact with some of them. Sometimes walls need to be climbed over or knocked down so we can live fully.

Later, I realized pulling back emotionally walled out the good with the bad. As I walled out the pain of relationships, I also walled out the benefits and the joys of relationships with those closet to me—and even to God. There are times for walls, and there are times when they need to come down.

When I was a child in third grade, I had not discovered that God had plans for me to overcome the obstacles and pain of my childhood. First though I had to learn that a relationship with God is the greatest treasure of all.

Chapter 3

Turquoise and Gold—
Discovering the Bactrian Hoard

The Worth of Finding God

The year was 1978; Dallas beat Denver in the Super Bowl 27–10. Norman Rockwell died. Three different Popes succeeded one another because of deaths, like a deck of cards falling in succession. The first test-tube baby, Louise Brown, was born, shocking the world and challenging the limits of human reproduction forever. Jimmy Carter held a conference at Camp David, with the president of Israel and the president of Egypt, where a historic document of peace between the nations was signed. Russian archeologist Vicktor Sarianidi unearthed in northern Afghanistan a 2,000-year-old treasure that would become known as the Bactrian Hoard.[2]

Sarianidi, following a King Midas legend of a "golden man buried in a coffin of gold,"[3] ended up on the outskirts of a quaint village in north-central Afghanistan. This legend led him four miles out of the town to the village of *Tillya Tepe,* when translated means "hill of gold."

He was looking for the ruins of a Persian fire temple. As he and his team began to dig, brushing away the earth grain by grain, gold coins and trinkets began to emerge. He soon realized that they hadn't only found a 4,000-year-old fire temple from ancient Persia, but a nomadic burial site bursting with gold.

Methodically, they continued to excavate, and late in the year 1978, six tombs lay bare; royalty from yesteryear collided with twentieth-century archeologists. Remains of five women in open coffins encircled a central tomb, which housed the remains of one man. The open coffins were each covered with a simple cloth adorned with silver and golden ornaments. What lay underneath these cloths is where legend grows to movie-like reality. Buried along with the corpses was approximately 21,000 pieces of gold trinkets, relics, jewelry, and artifacts from the ancient Bactrian Empire that spanned parts of Afghanistan, Tajikistan, and Uzbekistan. Alexander the Great tried and failed to conquer the Bactrian Empire in its entirety. The treasures found were from countries all across the Silk Road, and showed the vastness of trade that occurred in those days.[4]

Gold coins were found in the mouths of two of the women. In Greek mythology it was believed Charon, the ferryman of Hades, would guide the newly departed spirits across the river, for a price. His job was to take them from the world of the living to the world of the dead. At times coins were placed in the mouths of the dead to ensure they had money to pay this toll—a death fee.[5]

Golden bowls were found under the heads of several of the corpses, evidently to provide a golden cushion for them to rest upon for all eternity. The man, the protector of the group, was found with a golden belt around his waist, and attached to the belt were several swords strapped to his sides. Each sword had intricately designed golden hilts, embedded with turquoise.

An elaborate and delicate crown was found on one of the young women. Gold was hammered into small leaves, and flowers connected and intertwined to make a lightweight and ornamental headdress perhaps for a nomadic princess. Not only was it flashy, but it was functional. The crown could be disassembled so it could be slipped inside a goat-haired pouch and strapped to the back of a horse as they galloped across the ancient Silk Road.[6]

Heavy golden bracelets adorned their wrists and ankles, including boot buckles depicting chariots drawn by dragons embellished with turquoise; a golden trinket in the shape of an ibex; earrings, necklaces, golden scarabs; the list of jewelry and wealth goes on.

Systematically, Sarianidi and his team continued to dig and to classify all 21,000 pieces of the treasure. Due to the vastness of the treasure and its origins, it was named the Bactrian Hoard. They transported every last bit of it to the National Museum in Kabul. When it was found, political change was sweeping in. Russia invaded Afghanistan in 1979. Sarianidi and his companions could no longer work in peace or safety; thus he left Afghanistan and would not return again until he was an old man, more than a quarter of a century later.

The treasure stayed behind. Time marched on and the different artifacts from Afghanistan's past began to be sold on the black market. The Taliban raided the National Museum of Kabul and descended upon the housed artifacts.

Coins and other relics from Afghanistan began to appear in Britain, Japan, America, and it is rumored even on internet auction sites. By the 1990s, it was feared that the treasure had vanished, to be lost forever.

In time truth reveals itself, and stories that are worthy to be told start to emerge. By 2003, the buried treasure was ready to be rediscovered. Questions about it were asked again, and soon the world would discover the miracle of its recovery.

In 1989, the treasure was ordered to be moved from the museum, and placed in a vault underneath the Presidential Palace. Details seem to be hard to verify on this, but legend has it there were five or seven key holders to the vault. The *tawadars* were each given a key, and each of the keys had a lock it needed to fit into for the vault to open. If they were to pass away, the key should be passed on to their eldest son. During the time of the Taliban the key holders, who were the protectors of the treasure, were threatened and beaten, but none revealed the extent of their secret, nor was the vault ever successfully broken into.[7]

In the end, all the keys could not be found so a workman used various tools, a hammer, a crowbar, and a power saw to open the six different safes. It was all there. Every single golden coin, every trinket embedded with turquoise, and every article, wrapped in plastic and stored in locked chests. As rockets bombarded and destroyed buildings, as bullets peppered walls and windows, as homes and families were torn apart, the treasure laid deep underground.

For Afghanistan, the lost treasure being found symbolized hope and something glorious left after all the brokenness and terror. No amount of gold could ever restore the horrendous nightmares that many Afghans lived through during those days and make it palatable, but it was a physical symbol of something beautiful that had not been lost nor robbed by their adversaries. In those days, Afghanistan needed a lot of hope.

I don't know about you, but there are many days when I need a lot of hope, too.

* * *

Jesus told a story to a large crowd about a man who found a treasure. In this story he compared finding a treasure to finding the kingdom of God. The story went like this:

A man was digging in a field. As he dug, he came across something that wasn't a rock or a tree branch. He dug a little faster, and uncovered something beyond his wildest dreams…a vast treasure. He didn't own this field, so with great joy, he reburied the treasure and went home. In the story, Jesus said that he sold "everything." Perhaps, he sold his cow, his goat, his chickens, his house, his blankets, his kettle, his dishes, and the shirt off his back. We don't really know what he sold, but we do know that he was willing to give up everything so he could buy the field with the hidden treasure in it.

…Because, treasures are worth it, as is finding God.

* * *

As a child, every Sunday we went to a little Methodist church on Main Street in our small town. After the announcements, the organ thundered to life and the whole congregation stood in unison, clutching the red hymnal books inscribed with the Methodist logo of a cross with a flame. The congregation would heartily sing out three verses of "On Christ the Solid Rock I Stand," with the pastor kindly suggesting we skip the middle verse. Then, he cleared his throat and began...*Our Father, who art in heaven.* In unison, we all joined in without thought or hesitation. This was the warm-up for the Apostles' Creed...*I believe in God the Father Almighty, maker of heaven and earth, and in Jesus Christ His only son our Lord*...I soldiered on stumbling over a word or two, briefly wondering about different theological points in it, reciting along with the rest of the congregation... *the communion of saints, the forgiveness of sins, the resurrection of the body and the life everlasting. Amen.*

The whole thing took less than a minute to say. Both young and old all sat down with great gusto, worn out from the pledging and recitation of ancient texts. The pastor then had a time of prayer. The organ bellowed again, followed by time for the twenty-minute sermon, another hymn, and the closing benediction. The congregation slid out the long wooden pews and descended into the basement, the adults for percolated church-basement coffee and fellowship, while the kids headed for Sunday school.

Week after week, the routine of the service and the experience itself seldom varied. In Sunday school I, along with my sisters and a sparse number of other children, sat on hard metal chairs, and filled out papers with short stories on them about people in history that lived eons ago. They were interesting stories at first, but after a while it all seemed antiquated and irrelevant. It was what we did on Sundays, but it didn't help or give me any answers to my deep loneliness, nor my struggles at school. The stories became repetitive until one day, at the age of eleven, a simple question changed all of this.

"Melissa, do you want to go to summer camp?" my mother asked.

"Sure!"

It wasn't long before I had my bags packed, and I was ready to spend my first-ever week away from home. I ended up traveling to the weeklong family camp with an elderly farming couple, whose hearts were as big as their ample girth. They introduced me to Chinese food and truck-stop dining. We traveled farther north than I had ever been. After four or five hours, we finally rounded the bend and Lake Koronis emerged on the horizon. Its gray-blue waters whipped by the wind, waves lapped at the shore.

As we pulled into camp, I was then dropped off at the 4–6th grade girls' cabin. Not knowing what to expect, I hesitantly opened the cabin door and heard an eager voice say, "Come over here, you can have this bed!"

Two giggling girls greeted me with friendship and excitement. It was a weeklong encounter full of loving individuals of all ages, but Uncle Chuck was my favorite.

Uncle Chuck was in charge of the children's program. He was a short, stocky, grandfatherly-type man with a booming voice, who had a paint-brush and a head full of stories. As he told his stories, he would paint with bold, vibrant colors, and his brushstrokes magically turned into sunsets, block letters, and silhouettes.

When he spoke about Jesus, it was as if He mattered today.

I found out that knowing God was an actual choice. I didn't have to wait until I died to know if I was going to heaven like in the prayer I used to say every night as a young child.

> *Now I lay me down to sleep,*
> *I pray the Lord my soul to keep,*
> *If I die before I wake,*
> *I pray the Lord my soul to take.*[8]

I was always disturbed by the fact that I was acknowledging that I might not wake up in the morning, and God felt no closer before I prayed than after.

So I choose to follow God that week, and love and acceptance flowed into my heart. The love I had been searching for wrapped its comforting arms around me, and then squeezed.

It was a love that began to heal the brokenness that I felt from being bullied. The deep loneliness went away, and I discovered it didn't matter if I was *normal or not*. God loved me. So when Jesus tells the story of digging in the field, and selling everything you have for the kingdom of God, because it is like a treasure—I get it.

I would give the Afghan treasure, all 21,000 pieces of it, in all its beauty and splendor, for what I found at camp at age eleven.

I found my own life-changing treasure, my own Bactrian Hoard.

And, my faith grew and it ended up taking me places like Afghanistan, where I encountered God in the most unlikely of places at times, like the Buddhist monastery of Samangan.

Chapter 4

Caves of Samangan

The Search for the Celestial

Pausing for a moment, I craned my neck and stared straight up twenty-five feet before the azure sky emerged. Cold, hard granite sheered up to my left and another substantial circular stone wall curved to the right of me. My feet followed the path clockwise around a subterranean circular mound previously carved into the earth centuries prior by Buddhist Monks. This monastery near the city of Samangan in Northern Afghanistan pre-dates Islam.[9] It is one of the few testimonies of another religious era left in this country that has not been ravished and destroyed by invading armies, treasure thieves, and religious fanatics.

The year was early 2009, we had lived in Mazar-e-Sharif for the past three years, and a lot had changed in our family. Malcolm was now three years old, and during the summer of 2008 while we were back in America our daughter Emily joined our family.

The city of Samangan is a two-hour drive from Mazar and that day John, I, and the kids, along with several co-workers went to have a picnic and sightsee. After an al fresco lunch, we all went to explore the chambers of the monastery.

Treading deep on dry ground, an image flashed in my mind—a long line of shaven-headed monks in robes, plodding collectively and chanting in baritone unison. I imagined them meditating and probing their inner thoughts in an endless pursuit to answer the spiritual conundrum that has plagued human beings since our beginning. Why are we here? What were we created for? How do we as finite beings, encased and dwelling in bones and skin, connect with the infinite and spiritual world; a world that cannot even be seen.

Pacing around the loop again, I followed not my own path, but in the footsteps of the long dead. In awe of the amount of time, sheer grit and determination it must have taken to dig this immense circle into solid rock, a feeling of reverence descended on me. I thought of my own desire to pursue meaning and existence in a world, and how as a child I heard the whisper of the voice of God.

Emerging from the circular prayer chamber, I shifted six-month-old Emily to my other hip. We entered a long, low tunnel where small monastic meditation cells lined the walls. Grinning from ear to ear, Malcolm crawled into one, his youth touching the dirt of antiquity and dusting off the cobwebs of dreams whispered eons ago.

We continued to explore the other caverns, and then entered a large chamber where a detailed lotus flower was carved into the ceiling. The room had hollow crevices in the walls, which used to hold symbols of the Buddhist faith. A police officer in a khaki uniform asked for permission to take a photograph with Malcolm. He kneeled down, the photo was snapped and the flash bounced off the domed walls, radiating throughout the dark compartment, revealing the detail etched into each petal connecting and touching another.

As we emerged from exploring each chamber, a trail of curious children began to follow us foreigners. Wearing plastic sandals, they slipped on the rocks as they tried to keep up with us. We hiked straight up the steep rock enclave to visit the small building on top of the mound, which used to hold a statue of Buddha. This architecture was unique as Buddhist dome buildings are usually built above the ground, whereas this one in Samangan had been carved into the ground like the Coptic Churches in Ethiopia.

A narrow suspension bridge spanned the circular path below. I left blond-haired Malcolm and blue-eyed Emily behind with John, and crossed the bridge and took in the mountains that surrounded this monastery. The crimson mountains in the distance rose in spikes up from the flat, fertile plains. The brilliant red hue of the rock complemented the spring green, not unlike the Van Gogh painting, "Two Crabs," where the vibrant redness swims in an avocado sea of thick paint strokes. The morning haze lingered, adding to the delicate magnificence of this place, and I understood why a religious site had been built in this breathtaking area.

From the top of the mound, I spied women in sapphire burqas picnicking with their extended families, and the whiff of *Quabili Pilau*, a favored traditional rice dish, permeated the air. It was shortly after the New Year. In Afghanistan the New Year, *Nao Roz*, is celebrated on the equinox of March. The first day of the New Year ushers in the beginning of a month-long picnic season. Down the hill, the thumping beat of a *tabla* began, and teenage boys started to pulsate and stomp their feet to the tempo of the drum. Two worlds collided—one from the halls of old, thousands of years ago, another struggling to merge its recent violent past with the fragile promise of peace—and the enchantment and reverence of the place broke. Having been there for several hours, a large, curious crowd had begun to follow us. It was time to make the trek home.

Thinking about the monastery made me continue to reflect on humankind's search for meaning and purpose. Then another image that I frequently encountered in this Muslim land flashed into my mind.

During the summer months, as the warmth of the day dropped, from a window in my house I spotted an elderly man with a long white beard, wearing a turban on his head, and traditional long shirt and loose trousers, stooped down onto a prayer rug. He continued to worship slowly and methodically as the call to prayer reverberated in the air. There was a certain beauty and grace to his movements, and I prayed that he would find who he sought, worshiping in the way that he had been taught. He, like the ancient Buddhist monks of Samangan, pursued the age-old questions of how we as finite beings, made of molecules and cells, can connect with the infinite and eternal that we cannot even hear.

Our modern answer to this question is to say that God doesn't exist. Hoping if we ignore it, the innate sense that nags at all of us in the early morning's quiet—that we are missing out on something colossally important—will dissipate, like a sandcastle my children built too close to the sea.

* * *

God's whisper can catch you in the unexpected moments. It has me. When I was six, I got into trouble, fighting on the playground with my sister. Like a raging cub, I battled with my mother when she tried to sort out the fight. I was sent home with my father. Snuffling all the time we walked up to our house, I was in sheer terror about what kind of punishment I would get. My dad, a man of few words, marched me all the way up the long hill. When we went inside, he sat me down on a couch, turned away, walked toward the refrigerator, cracked open a can of grape soda and handed it to me. That was it: *God's grace.*

Once when we were young, my sisters and I spotted a crayfish swimming in the little stream we used to play in among the hills. We spent what seemed like hours trying to catch it in the yellow sand pail we had brought along. Finally my sisters, Julie and Jolyn, and I proudly marched home carrying it in a little bucket. We went upstairs, filled up the bathtub and let it loose. To our astonishment, the crayfish swam backwards: *God's design.*

Rushing home after school, I opened the door and saw my mother at the top of our stairs. "Your father has been taken to rehab by Uncle Larry." At age nine, rehab meant nothing to me, but I sensed some sort of miraculous thing had happened as joy and lightness filled my mother's voice. Our house was quiet for a month, and then he returned, and for all my childhood years, he remained sober: *God's restoration.*

As a teenager, I traveled with a church group to Botswana, where on the dusty soil of the Kalahari Desert, I watched the sun began to set, the horizon stretching endlessly from east to west, and the stars began to appear, like Christmas lights twinkling on and off. Transfixed, far from a world of light pollution, I understood I was a part of something divine: *God's creation.*

Another time, as I was driving home from the movies with my younger brother, Michael, a shock ran through my body as the thud of a giant mammal collided with the front of the car. In slow motion, a deer careened over the windshield at the same time peace descended on me, and the unspoken comforting words washed over me, "everything is okay, you'll be alright": *God's protection.*

Years later as I cradled my newly birthed son, John, my husband and amazing birth coach was by my side. Our eyes absorbed this new life. The baby was now breathing, revived by the neonatal resuscitation team, fragile, intricate, and looking like he was wearing my nose. Conceived after a year of trying, carried for what felt like the length of an elephant's pregnancy, I realized we had brought forth life from our love: *God's miracle.*

And treading in a clockwise direction deep in the ground in a land far from my native home, I thought of the monks that hewed this out of stone, and I knew why they did it—they heard the call of the Celestial.

Because, so do I.

I learned it is in the everydayness of life that God speaks to us, and it was in the everydayness of life in Afghanistan that I continued to glean truths about His purposes and His character.

Chapter 5

The Myth of the Mourning Doves

Folktales and the Reality of Truth

A snow-white dove alighted on the peak of a seagreen-and-blue tiled mosque that was glistening in the sun. She paused for a slight second, all movement ceasing in her agile body, and then her feathers vibrated slightly and her milky wings spread out to touch the indigo sky. Swooping down, she joined hundreds of other shimmering and moon-colored doves that make this shrine in the northern city of Mazar-e-Sharif their home.

Legend says when a grey dove, perhaps one of the abundant mourning doves found in Afghanistan, relocates to the shrine within thirty days of residence, then they will magically shed their dusky-colored feathers for a frock of pure white.

Indeed, besides the multi-colored ducks living in the manmade ponds, a significant number of these white doves dwell around this enchanted shrine. The Blue Mosque would be a fitting place for a story straight out of the Arabian Nights, its beauty and example of Islamic artwork is spectacular as is its historical significance. Instead of flying carpets, at night the shrine is decorated with strings of colorful holiday lights and a neon sign reading "Hazrat-e-Ali" in the Arabic script, the perfect background for the street vendors selling pureed juices and carrot smoothies.

In the springtime, The Festival of the Red Tulips, *Gul-e-Surkh*, is celebrated in Mazar, and thousands of pilgrims travel to this holy site where Ali, the nephew of the Prophet, is believed to be buried. The city takes on a festive and carnival-like feel, and the population doubles and triples. It grows bloated, ready to pop like the buttons of a shirt worn by a man who won't come to grips with his middle-aged expanding body.

The festival starts with the first day of the Afghan New Year, *Nao Roz*, and the celebration begins with the raising of the *Janda* pole, a towering flagpole which is erected in the center of the park around the Blue Mosque.

It is whispered that if you are sick, if you can be the first person to touch the top of the flagpole as it is being raised, your sickness will dissipate, your disease will be cast off, and your body restored. Each year a substantial crowd gathers around the pole, and the bodies push, strain, and jostles each other, vying for the most prime positions as the pole is raised. Each year, others stay away, fearful that they will be trampled in the mass of people, or their children lost in the shuffle.

So much of Afghan culture has folklore and legends weaved into facts of everyday life. Some of these beliefs are harmless, while others are deadly.

A doctor who worked at a local provincial hospital told me the story of a severely dehydrated newborn that had been brought into the emergency room with bloody diarrhea and loose stools. When the mother was questioned, her story of heartbreak and desperation tumbled out.

She had lost three previous children from natural causes in their first few weeks of life. When she became pregnant with this child, she was determined to do something so it would live. A friend of hers traveled to Mecca, to the spring of *Zam Zam*. This friend brought back a small fragment of rock from this hallowed spring. The mother ground it to a powder and fed it to her newborn. She so urgently wanted to instill life into his fragile body. Indeed, her intervention did the exact opposite.

Her decision was not a rational one. She was working out of a completely different worldview and framework than our own. She had moved from a rational belief to a magical framework.

The world that Jesus walked in existed between these two extremes.

The time Jesus walked on the earth was before modern medicine and good healthcare. People died prematurely from sickness and diseases, and doctors offered little hope. Jesus, who had power over diseases, drew such large crowds it became dangerous for him to walk freely about because so many wanted his healing touch.

Jesus' ministry did not deal with only healing and restoration from sickness of the body, but it also dealt with the spirit world. He and his disciples spiritually restored many individuals who had been tormented and traumatized by demons and the dark world.

In Afghanistan, they are called *jinn*.

Jinn are either mischievous beings that play tricks on people, or beings of malevolence who bestow adversity, disease, and suffering on unsuspecting people. Many people live in great fear of jinn. They are terrified to sleep alone in a room. Lights are left on all night (if the electricity isn't cut off), verses of the Koran or talismans are pinned on children to keep them safe, and charcoal is used as eyeliner, especially on babies, to ward off the evil eye. It is not unusual for a *mullah*, the religious teachers, to make charms and cast spells to keep evil spirits away.

Some people deny the existence of these jinn, but they still appear in stories and in popular legends. One day our office was all in an uproar. Someone discovered all the employees were circulating a picture that one of our engineers had on his mobile. He claimed it was a picture of a jinn. Our teachers, other engineers, and office managers were all eagerly viewing and confirming that it could only be such a thing.

Since the birth of Christianity, the religion has gone through periods of its own folklore and legendary beliefs. Historical church leaders have been known to mix myth with truth to the detriment of its followers.

During the middle ages, there was a fervent fascination with relics. The search for the Holy Grail, the seamless tunic Jesus wore on the cross, the cross of thorns he bore on his head, and the sale of pieces of the original cross that Christ was crucified on, were all objects highly sought after and desired. It was believed that owning such objects brought favor, blessing and miracles upon the possessors of such artifacts.[10] Some of these objects are on display today in cathedrals or in Rome, and visitors still flock to see them, although their authenticity remains unproven.

In the Middle Ages, the cathedrals or monasteries that held these items became places of pilgrimage. People would pay money to the church to visit and see these items, hoping for a miracle by being able to be close in proximity to them. These physical earthly objects, whether fabrications or the real images, brought something tangible to people who desperately wanted to feel, see, and touch the spiritual world. During those times, the Bible was taught and recited in a foreign language, Latin. Those who attended church regularly had no idea if the truth was being taught or not. They looked to their spiritual leaders to connect them to the divine, and the leaders used folklore and superstition to exploit their followers.

In today's world, we may laugh at these things, but there are areas in society and in our beliefs where we still behave based on superstitions. Thirteen is the unlucky number; some airplanes and hospitals skip over it like it doesn't exist. We teach our children to wish upon the stars...*I wish I may, I wish I might have this wish I wish tonight.* Also, we teach them to make wishes when they blow candles out on their birthday. Don't tell your wish though, or it might not come true.

Sometimes, the boogieman comes up in conversation directed towards a misbehaving child. Beliefs prevail about good luck charms like four-leaf clovers, and a common phrase we hear is "beginner's luck." Even sports teams like the Chicago Cubs had stories about curses passed down for years that justified their inability to win the World Series for over a hundred years. In football, we use terms like Hail Mary for scoring against unbelievable odds.

Most of these beliefs and sayings are simply for fun, and we don't really believe them. Yet, superstitious beliefs can filter into our faith and beliefs in God. Some may be harmless, but others may cause us to stop believing in God when we are disappointed and don't get what we desire.

As Christians we may have a favorite verse we use like a mantra, if we repeat it often enough perhaps, like magic, we will get what we want. How about the belief…if I do good things, good things will happen to me. "Pay it forward" has become a popular concept. "God doesn't want me to suffer" or "God wants me to be happy" can be very hard beliefs to reconcile when we face difficult times. How do we filter out truth from popular teachings?

Jesus' words are recorded in the New Testament saying, "We must be as gentle as doves, but as wise as serpents." The Biblical scholars and pastors in our lives help keep us grounded. When we read God's word for ourselves, and earnestly search for his truth, we discover truth. I remember a time when I first made an effort to read, not only bits and pieces of the Bible, but to read it in its entirety. When I hit the lengthy parts…I froze.

I prayed. "I don't think I can do this, God. I don't think I will ever get through this dull book!"

Then something miraculous happened. The words and messages started to become mesmerizing. Over the months that I read the Bible, I encountered the God of the universe, the God of the traveler, the God of a widow named Ruth, the cries of a king, the brokenness of humanity, the songs of the exiled, the plans of builders, the shouts of victors, the sobs of mothers, encounters with angels, the birth of a babe, the teachings of a Savior, the betrayal of friends, the gift of forgiveness, a knock at a door, hope restored, a people united, lives changed, and a vision of the future. Through these times a deep abiding trust in God grew in me, and it wasn't a magical framework that I believed in, but a concrete one. Through these stories, I found living truth and a loving God.

Chapter 6

Tenacity—In the Hands of a Nation

God's Gift of Prayer

My co-worker and I sat in an office waiting for our turn to speak with the director of nursing. We were waiting to obtain permission to work with the nurses' school on site at the Provincial Hospital. The day was sweltering and arid like many days in Mazar, but that isn't what made it awkward.

The ornate office sported beautiful gold curtains and an intricate Persian carpet—despite the fact that half of the hospital was only charred remains from a raging fire. As a result of the fire, the women's ward and pediatric units were shoved into side rooms, makeshift tents, and hallways. The rumor circulated that the director of the hospital, in the pursuit of wanting aid money to build a bigger and more elaborate office and hospital facility, started the fire himself. Perceiving that the nursing director's office would make a better temporary ward than the outside tents, I thought maybe the nursing director was in cahoots with the hospital director.

As we waited for the person before us to complete his business and get his paper signed, I pulled at my headscarf and tried to adjust it back into place. Headscarves are slippery things, and since I didn't grow up wearing one, it didn't come naturally to me—and I didn't have the grace and ease the women around me demonstrated as they donned them like a second skin. The trick was to get it back into an appropriate place without actually taking it off, exposing your naked hair, which of course would be a horrendous thing to do in the presence of so many men. That day I wanted to rip off my head covering, free my hair, and then put it back into place. It was the very thing everything inside of me was screaming to do, but none of those things were what made it awkward.

The awkwardness came from a petite grandmother-type woman sitting in the corner of the room, wearing a traditional white headscarf that was appropriate for a woman her age to wear. It was a headscarf of importance and a headscarf of dignity.

As the Director of Nursing addressed the people approaching his desk, this elderly woman continued to interrupt him from the corner of the room with a request for a job for her son. Due to her age, the director kindly replied that there were no jobs available at the moment for her son, and then turned his attention to the person who scheduled a meeting with him.

The elderly woman wasn't deterred. She went on about how it was nonsense, the hospital was a big place with many jobs, and she only wanted one job for her son. The director ignored her for a while, and then patiently replied that there were no jobs available for her son.

This continued for some time. Finally it was our turn, but before we could start, the elderly woman repeated her request. The tension in the room was palpable as I saw the director sigh, obviously worn down by this woman's tenacity. Then with a firm voice, he repeated how it was impossible for him to give her son a job, and it was time for her to leave. He turned to us, and we explained our proposal for working with the nursing school.

He welcomed our ideas to be volunteer staff to assist with the nursing school clinicals at the hospital. From our observations gathered from volunteering as nurses at the hospital and from observing the nursing program, we learned the content of what the student nurses were taught was current information. Yet, when they came to the hospital they were unsupervised and not given any opportunity to apply their new knowledge. A crucial step in transitioning from a student nurse to a graduate nurse is to become confident in bedside skills. My co-worker and I would be additional nursing supervisors for the students' clinicals, since the current ratio of teachers to students was too large. He graciously accepted our offer, and a start date was set up. We were also informed that we should wear a white coat and a small head covering.

During this whole process, the elderly woman remained. She apparently hadn't given up. We finished speaking, and as we left I heard her pipe up again, repeating her request along with her story of woe, and the need for someone in her household to have a job.

I never saw her again, but somehow I think eventually someone in her household was granted a job at the hospital that day. In the end, I believe her persistence won him over. It reminded me of the story of another elderly lady, the Parable of the Persistent Widow:

> *Jesus told his disciples the following story: "In a certain city there was a judge who neither feared God nor respected man. And there was a widow in that city who kept coming to him and saying, 'Give me justice against my adversary.' For a while he refused, but afterwards he said to himself, "Though I neither fear God nor respect man, yet because this widow keeps bothering me, I will give her justice, so that she will not beat me down by her continual coming."*
> —Luke 18:2-5

Tenacity and persistence are words I have come to understand better after living in Afghanistan. It seems to be a cultural value. From the beggar on the street, to the children who wanted to come and play in my yard, to the representative who came looking for jobs for those connected to their families, they all seem to possess this inner drive that if they ask enough times, surely, "yes" will eventually be the answer.

I can't tell you the number of times I'd hear a knock on my gate, and when I answered it, eight smiling neighbor kids would be standing in front of the gate. They loved our yard because we had swings, soccer balls, and several scooters they used on the sidewalk we had intentionally connected together into a square so they could loop around over and over again. Sometimes I would bring out coloring books and crayons for them too. Many of the neighborhood children were sent outside on the street to play because their mothers were busy cooking and cleaning, and they wanted them out of the way.

I didn't mind them coming and playing. But I wanted to be in control as to when and at what times they came. This was a hard lesson to teach.

"Can we come and play for a minute?"

"No, not now, my daughter is sleeping, it isn't a good time."

"But, *Khola jan* (Auntie)," they pleaded, using the polite term used to address women.

"Can't we come for five minutes?"

"No, I am afraid she will wake up."

"Oh, we can be really quiet; we want to play for five minutes. Please..."

Eyeing the eight children standing there I knew they would quickly forget about being quiet. "Can't you come back this afternoon?"

"No, we have school." "No, my mother needs my help." "No, I have to study."

"Can't we come for a little bit?"

"No," I said. "My daughter is sleeping, she gets grumpy when she is woken up."

"But, we will be really quiet. Let us come in and play for just five minutes."

After this typical conversation, two things either happened: I gave up and let them come and play or I would shut the gate because they wouldn't accept my reasoning. Leaving them standing there, somehow I always felt like I was the loser.

Another example of this is the teenage neighbor girl who wanted to study abroad in Turkey. She was convinced practicing her English with me every chance she got would help her with her studies abroad. I didn't mind practicing English with her, but she always seemed to pop up at the most inconvenient times. She showed up at my house at noon for a language lesson right when I had begun to cook lunch. I tried explaining to her that I needed to get lunch ready for my family.

She was not deterred, "I can wait."

I had to be a bit more direct. "No, this time isn't good at all, you have to pick another time."

"I can come at four," and then she proceeded to come every day at four. I agreed to this time commitment knowing it would be difficult, but she had told me she was going to go to Turkey in two weeks' time. So I thought it would be short-lived.

Four months later, she still hadn't left.

She faced multiple obstacles and rejections from the authorities in obtaining a visa to study abroad. She and her father persisted, and she continued coming for her English lessons.

After four months, I discussed with John the fact that I should probably help her come to the reality that she should focus her energy on getting into medical college here in Afghanistan. However, through her persistence, she finally boarded a plane with the proper documentation to begin the arduous journey of first learning Turkish, and then finding a medical school to attend.

She would have understood the woman's persistence in Jesus' story, because she never would have settled for anything short of what she felt she should do.

Widows during Jesus' time would have been like widows in present-day Afghanistan. Women whose husbands die do not get their husband's property, and they usually have no means to support themselves. Even their children, birthed from their own bodies, are considered property of the husband's family. When their husband dies, many times they lose everything.

They, in many ways, are an embodiment of the word *powerless*. The widow in this story possessed a knowledge she was in the right, and she had been part of an unjust situation. In the end, it was her tongue that gave her the greatest advantage, and the knowledge that the judge possessed the power to change her situation and give her what she deserved.

In fact, in many situations we are the widow in this story. Our child becomes addicted to drugs, our spouse has an affair, we hate our jobs, we remain childless, mental illness rears its ugly head, terrorism arrives at our front doorstep, and we don't know how to change any of it. Waves of powerlessness overwhelm us.

Luke 18:1 stated:
And he told them a parable to the effect that they ought always to pray and not lose heart.

Who hasn't lost heart in one situation or the next? In our case, God is the encourager who can make all the difference in our lives, and it is a welcome invitation to bother God anytime and anywhere about the issues that are bothering us. This is simply one aspect of God's character though. As I read the Bible, I learned that God has many facets to His personality, like being the humble king.

Chapter 7

Donkeys and Demigods

A Worthy King

Four hundred years of silence...no prophetic words, no Messiah, no written evidence that God's people had not been abandoned. There were 400 years of silence between the time Malachi, the last book of the Old Testament, was written and before the birth of Christ, the promised Messiah. The prophets' mouths and spirits were stilled, waiting for their redeemer.

When Jesus walked on the earth, the Jewish nation lived under the oppressive thumb of the Roman government. The elderly, the very young, the middle-aged, and the teenagers prayed for a time when they could be free to dictate their own laws, run their own country, and freely worship their God. A word, *Messiah...savior* circulated, like the Israelites enslaved in Egypt so long ago, the Jewish nation groaned under the oppressive government and prayed for a liberator of their nation. Indeed, Zechariah, John's father, prophesied after the birth of his son, that we should be saved from our enemies and from the hand of all who hate us. —Luke 1:71

Long, long ago before the whispered promises of a Savior spread throughout the Jewish community, the nation of Israel was kingless; God was to be their king. But, they wanted to be like all the other countries around them. They cried out for a king, but God warned them of the nature of the human heart. He warned them of the hardships a human king would bring—the king would send their sons off to war to fight for his kingdom, and they would have to fill the king's coffers before they filled their own bellies.

The Israelites rejected God as their king. God let them have their own way (like He often does), and the nation of Israel was given a king. It wasn't long before all warnings came to pass. The nation divided and encountered great sorrow, and during the time Jesus walked the earth, they lived under the oppressive Roman regime. Whispers and hopes abounded that someday their deliverer would sweep in and save them from their daily torment.

* * *

Fast-forward two thousand plus years to a small city near the Hindu Kush...

A cloud of dust billows out from under the hooves of a mob of galloping horses. The powder-fine dirt permeates the air as the horses increase their speed. Their riders urge them on with whips, and the sounds of pulsating hooves echoes throughout the cheering crowd. Despite the fact they were running on hard, packed dirt, the stampede of stallions creates a jarring sounds. Amidst the chaos, from among the crowded group of riders, a victor emerges, and one of the *Chapandaz* who's wearing a thick cloth coat and leather helmet, stands tall. His feet strain against the leather stirrups. He rears his horse, breaks free from the spirited herd, and in his hand he drags the prize, a rope with a black beheaded calf, around a very tall flagpole erected at the end of the field. He then in one fell swoop tosses the calf into a chalked white circle, and raises his fist in victory.

The crowd's mighty voices resonate off the nearby mountains in one united roar, like a mighty rushing river. From the women's section, a large number of veiled women standing on buildings and sitting on the far hillsides clap and cheer, though none sit close because *Buzkashi* is a man's game.

Before moving to Afghanistan I had never heard of the game *Buzkashi*. After moving there, I was intrigued by the game. I learned that *Buzkashi* is their national sport and pride. The country has an Olympic committee that continues to put forward a request to have *Buzkashi* made an Olympic sport. This belief was so strong that in Faizabad where we lived for several years, a new metal fence was erected around the Buzkashi field, and it was painted blue, and the Olympic rings adorned its gates.

As I watched the game, I was transported back through the centuries. It was not hard to imagine Genghis Khan himself, sitting on the rock-formed stadium seats that surround the field, wielding a sword and placing his own bets on the champion. It is an intense game of power and brute force. The object of the game is to capture the body of a beheaded calf or goat attached to a rope, and drag it around the flagpole for points. *Buzkashi* translated literally means "goat pulling."

The central figure of the sport is the *Chapandaz*, the rider and the hero of the game. If their skill and popularity grow across the country, they rise to a form of fame and godlike status not unlike professional athletes in our own countries. The name Aziz Ahmad, one of the most famous Buzkashi players, is revered and treated with admiration and pride in many households, the same as Michael Jordan or Babe Ruth.

These *Buzkashi* professionals are often supported by powerful warlords that provide them both horses and an excellent salary. The warlords in turn gamble on their backed *Chapandaz,* often thousands of dollars, and so it is not only a spectator sport, but a deadly game of odds and victors.

* * *

The Jewish nation during the time of Jesus was not unlike any other oppressed group in the world. The nation craved and yearned for a leader to rise up who would begin a movement of liberation to lead their people out of physical bondage and oppression. They placed their hopes on a star, not unlike our modern sports figures, not unlike the *Chapandaz* sitting tall on a stallion, full of charisma and danger.

In rode a man…a mere wood carver…straddling a half-grown donkey…

When I entered rural life in Afghanistan I discovered that it is chock-full of donkeys. Donkeys are docile creatures in contrast to the stallion that is the animal of choice for *Buzkashi*. After watching the donkeys for a while, it is easy to see why they are preferred for this hard and mountainous land. They are able to be used for numerous tasks. During the time we lived in Faizabad, I watched hundreds of donkeys make the long trip down the side of a mountain to the local water pipe with boys and lemon-colored water containers upon their backs. They also were used to haul loads of sand in twin black saddle bags up from the river beds to be used in construction, and at other times they carried elderly men who sat astride them, their feet only inches off the ground, using them like we use automobiles.

Malcolm, and then later, Emily played, "The Donkey Counting Game." At certain times a year, I would have them sit by our upstairs kitchen window and keep track of all the donkeys that passed by our house on their way to the river to get sand for building materials. Back and forth they would go, and the count would grow.

Before encountering so many donkeys, when I had read about the Messiah riding in on a young donkey on Palm Sunday, I pictured him riding slowly on a short, dusky-colored animal with long ears. I didn't grasp the importance of Jesus riding a donkey—or the irony of it.

The horse is an animal of royalty, of sports, and a symbol of power. Traditionally the horse was an animal used in war. It was an animal fit for kings. The *Chapandaz* were able to afford to ride because powerful warlords own the horses. The Egyptian army that was mounted on their horses and in their chariots were chasing after the escaping Israelites that were fleeing on foot. Well, that's certainly powerful imagery. Whoever heard of an army riding to battle on donkeys?

Donkeys are animals of labor, and those who own them are laborers. Jesus' gesture of riding on a humble donkey through the streets on Passover emphasized the point that the kingdom he was ushering in was a kingdom of peacemakers, a kingdom of reconciliation, and a kingdom for the everyday. He was identifying with the laborer—not the wealthy or the powerful.

This is what I have always loved about the heart of God's story. The creator of galaxies and goldfish, roses and rhinoceros, mold and Mount Everest, sent Jesus to dwell in a mother's womb for nine months, to be born in a stable, and grow up in a typical house. Despite his low status, Jesus influenced history for thousands of years, and continues to do so even today.

Had he come as their physical liberator, he would have long been forgotten in the eroding pages of history. He would have simply been another name in a long list of leaders that school children would have repeated and had to memorize—but he was so much more than this.

It doesn't make sense, but it gives me hope. Jesus' mission wasn't political freedom; it was about freedom of the heart. It wasn't about physical victories; it was about spiritual ones. It wasn't about being the *Chapandaz*; it was about being accessible, and it wasn't about making a difference at one point in time; it was about making a difference forever.

That's the God I want to have, and as a child, this accessible humble God is who I discovered, and accepted His love, really without question. As I grew older though, sometimes I would forget the beauty and joy of His love.

Chapter 8

Cucumber Sandwiches and Paintbrushes

Rediscovering How to Approach God

I was given a gift during my time in Afghanistan. For the four years when my children were preschool age, I helped run and co-teach at a preschool for expatriate and Afghan children. During that time, I learned many lessons from these preschoolers, but the most precious lesson was something I think anyone who works with children probably understands.

The paintbrush swirled around in the water, the red color turned the water a pale pink. Then the painter lifted it out again and dipped it into the brilliant red on the chunky paint palette. Larissa, a lithe young girl of six with golden hair, dragged the brush across the large white paper with skilled precision. Using one curving stroke after another, she soon created an oversized and brightly colored gul, a flower. I watched her painting and smiled, as she hummed softly, lost in the land of childhood.

One day I visited Larissa's home with my German friend, Mirjam.

Larissa is the last child of six; four girls and two boys. At her birth, when she came out with lighter skin and blonde hair, her parents chose to give her a Greek name. In parts of Afghanistan you can find both blue and green-eyed Afghans, with red or blond hair. These Afghans trace their genetic traits back to the time when Alexander the Great, along with his Grecian troops, marched across the land.

Larissa's family lived in a three-room mud house with a small, enclosed garden, which had grape vines, pomegranate trees, and chickens. Her father was a guard who makes less than two hundred dollars a month. Her mother and father were illiterate until the previous year when they both enrolled in courses and learned to read for the first time. Though they were uneducated, they sent all of their children to school—the boys *and* girls.

"I'll go and make the tea," the mother said, and left the room.

The three other children in the room stared back at me. Adeeb, Larissa's ten-year-old brother, erupted into a grin.

"My mother used to ride a camel."

"Really?" I replied, smiling.

Adeeb continued. "When she was a child, she grew up where there are many rivers, fish, and camels. She fished and swam, and sometimes got to ride a camel." He became excited, and I could tell he relished this fact about his mother.

The other children were now chiming in telling us things about their mother's extraordinary adventures. I thought about their mother, long ago as a child mounted upon a great beast riding in green places. This is the same woman, who when she exits her gate, always pulls down a long blue cloth, the burqa, that clings and hides her body, her face, her essence. This woman, who happened to be only slightly older than me, was the mother of six children, but she had also returned newborn babies to the earth because they never took that first life-breath.

Later, she came with the customary green tea, dish of pistachios, almonds, and raisins. As she poured out our tea, my friend and I asked her if she had enjoyed her camel rides. She laughed heartily, and then related to us how she had a "free" childhood running here and there until she was married at the age of fourteen. As her memories of childhood faded away, she became quieter, and when her children left the room, she spoke to us about her recent miscarriage of a baby boy.

When we are children, the fears and challenges we face tower over us, but we live in the hope that when we obtain the sought-after land of adulthood, all our troubles will slip away. As children, we believe we will be free to do what we want, and we'll be in control of our own fates.

That day at preschool, Larissa finished her painting and hung it up with two clothespins outside to dry in the sun. When she came in, I announced, "Snack time!" Ramon, Abdullah, Shamisa and her twin sister Parmin, Tara, Emily, Elias, and several others tumbled over each other, rushing to the door to go and wash their hands. They raced back and scrambled around the traditional plastic tablecloth Afghans roll out on the floor and use for eating at instead of a table, jostling continuously as they settled into position. I passed out whole cucumbers and knives, and they gleefully and viciously hacked them into irregular bits. I kept a keen eye on anyone who decided to use his or her knife as a weapon. One by one, the cucumber slices were thrown onto a tray.

Larissa got out the salt and sprinkled it all over the dark-green juicy sections. Azita, a girl with a short bobbed hair, munched on one and commanded, "It tastes bad, put on more salt." I quickly intercepted before the cucumbers were swimming in a briny sea. The preschoolers with their stubby fingers ripped pieces of naan, the flatbread Afghans love, wrapped cucumbers inside it, and feasted.

One of our preschoolers from America, announced, "When I grow up I am going to make naan and cucumber sandwiches at McDonald's."

"That would be wonderful," I replied, grinning.

The children devoured their snacks, raced to the door, struggled to put their shoes on, several leaving sandal straps unhinged while they whipped outside as fast as their short legs could take them. They sprinted to get to the trampoline first. They could jump four at a time, and everyone would have a turn. Each one hefted his or her little body up onto the giant trampoline and bounced. Up, down, back and forth, they shrieked and giggled, and I took pleasure in watching their great joy.

One day as Jesus was busy healing and preaching, several parents brought their little children to him for a blessing. The disciples, practical men, sent the parents and children away, telling them he was too "busy" for such trivial things. Jesus overheard their rebuke, called the children to him, and said, *"Let the little children come to me and do not hinder them, for to such belongs the kingdom of heaven."* —Matthew 19:14

As a mother and a preschool teacher, I learned little children have a lot of flaws. They frequently urinate near, but not in the toilet. They think the floor is the best place to spread every single toy they own. They smear foods like spaghetti sauce, Jell-O, and oatmeal over their squat little faces. They get up at every inconceivable hour of the night. They whine. They cry. They scream. They let running mucus drip down their faces. They drop your toothbrush in the toilet and forget to tell you about it. They chew with their mouths open. They lose their mittens. They vomit on your new purse, and they ask a thousand unanswerable questions with one word: *Why?*

Sometimes, I find it hard to believe that Jesus says that the kingdom of heaven belongs to imperfect creatures like this.

In contrast, little children have a lot of strengths. Their laughs and giggles are laced with fluffy cotton candy and pixie dust. Little children have a dogged energy to discover the world around them. They get excited by the everyday things of life: watching a caterpillar climbing up a tree, stomping through mud puddles in a pair of rain boots, being allowed to chew bubble gum, smelling and picking wildflowers, catching snowflakes on the tip of their tongues, mixing up sand and water with a yellow plastic shovel, dragging their feet through the crunchy fading leaves of autumn, petting the cat's fur the wrong way, and the excitement of getting pushed on a swing.

Children know how to live in the present, to enjoy the everydayness of life.

As adults, we usually have lost the wonders and excitement of being in the land of our imagination, and the pleasure one can take in painting a large red flower. We have grown up, and our childhoods have evaporated into cirrus clouds. Too often we have lost our dreams of making cucumber and naan sandwiches, because our reality-saturated lives have stolen our most precious gift of all—hope—with our relentless schedules and constant stream of bills. We have forgotten how to believe that *tomorrow will be a better day.*

Can you imagine a little child on God's lap, talking and asking questions? God, how did you make the whole world? Why did you let the dinosaurs die? Why don't I have a baby sister or brother? Can I have a snack? Do you want to play LEGOs with me? Watch me twirl! Do you like my picture? Guess what, I pooped in the potty. My mom loves this. I got a chocolate. Do you want to hear the craziest thing—my mom, she is older than my dad, but she is so much shorter than him? I don't get it. Did you know when I was just born, I screamed, and then the doctor cut my vocal cords. But, it didn't hurt.

Children don't have all the answers, *but they still know how to believe.* Is this what Jesus meant? I realized that sometimes, God wants me to be ridiculous and believe, too. Who knows… this could mean that God might want me to giggle while bouncing on a giant trampoline, to paint a large red flower, or to make cucumber sandwiches at McDonald's. Or perhaps, God wants me to wake up each day with hope in my heart and delight in the fact that I am alive.

Part of having child-like faith has to do with freedom. Children are able to quickly forgive, they may throw a temper tantrum after being told "No!" but after a twenty-minute nap, they usually love that person as if nothing happened.

As adults we have long memories; however, being able to live in the present has a lot to do with discovering that God has given us *the ability to forgive*—to be able to move forward—forgetting the past so that we can dream again.

Chapter 9

Meat for Eating and Ritual Sacrifices

A Lesson in Forgiveness

Turning the corner in the bustling bazaar, I stopped abruptly. Gingerly I stepped over three sheep heads resting on the gritty sidewalk curb. Lopped off at the neck, their glazed and stunned eyes locked with mine. Shuddering, I continued on past the rows of meat hooks with dead carcasses hanging, ready for the day's customers. Being early spring, the flies were few, but at the height of mid-summer, they swarm in huge numbers and engulf the carcasses, feasting on the free flesh. We tended to be vegetarians early June through late September.

Not all the meat for sale in the bazaar was already dead. Fat chickens in wire cages stacked on top of each other lined the pavement, waiting for the customer who found a fresh fowl was needed when uninvited guests dropped in for a mid-day meal. Occasionally, a steer tied up with a rope chewed its cud as it waited to be slaughtered.

The meat section is not for the faint of heart. In the west, we cannot appreciate the effort and energy that goes into the cubed, ground, sliced, and diced meat wrapped in plastic and Styrofoam that we toss so easily into our metal carts. These packages disguise the truth about where meat originates, which makes it easy to forget that it comes from living, breathing beings.

Food suppliers spend many hours packaging up and marketing desires, slapping labels on them and calling them by a different name than what they really are. The truth is evaded, like for the children who don't know milk really comes from cows, or chicken nuggets actually come from real birds.

Raising animals for food and butchering is a way of life for many Central Asians. So is killing them for religious purposes. This is most evident during the festival of sacrifice, *Eid-e-Qorban*, a holiday that is celebrated on a rotating lunar calendar like Easter.

The prices of sheep skyrocket right before *Eid-e-Qorban*, and herds of baaing sheep, their backs marked with red and pink colors to indicate who their owners are, begin to be shepherded into the city limit to the bazaar to be sold and then slaughtered at home.

It is the biggest festival in Afghanistan, which stems from a story the three major world religions—Christianity, Islam, and Judaism—still observe in some way.

Eid-e-Qorban is the celebration of when God provided a great sacrifice in the place of Abraham's son.[11] God asked Abraham to take his son and sacrifice him on an altar. Abraham trusted God, so he packed his cart, loaded it with wood, and set off on a three-day journey with his son in tow. Each morning Abraham would have arisen early as the sun crested over the horizon to continue on this journey of grave peril. Did Abraham lie awake looking at the stars in the sky, remembering the promise that God had given him so long ago? …"Abraham, someday your descendants would be as numerous as the stars."

Each day, he could have turned back, each day he could have said, "God, it is too much." But, he persisted, because he loved God. When he and his son arrived at the chosen spot, he tied him to an altar, but when he raised his knife, an angel appeared, halting the terrible tragedy that could have been. The angel let Abraham know this was only a test of his loyalty, and then a sacrificial ram was provided.

Therefore, during *Eid-e-Qorban*, people continue to sacrifice animals.

If you have enough money, you buy a sheep, a cow, a yak, or even a camel to sacrifice on the day of preparation. That day, the head of the animal is held back, causing the neck to be exposed, the jugular veins of the animal throb and one of the members of the family first says a prayer, and then takes a large knife and slashes the throat. The blood gushes forth, and the life of the animal wilts away.

In Afghanistan, the ritual has little to do with forgiveness, but it has to do with honoring God and earning *sawab*, which is merit or earning favor with God. If you sacrifice an animal, you get a lot of approval from God, especially if it is a large animal like a cow, yak, or a camel. In the end, they hope it is possible for some to have earned enough merit to successfully balance out the bad things one has done.

In Badakhshan, where we lived for about four years, they mostly sacrifice indigenous Afghan Karakul sheep, and a special stew is prepared from these fat-tailed sheep. The fat of the *dumba* (backside) is popular in Persian and Arab cooking. The meat is fried in the tail-fat along with some onions, and rice is added to make a gelatinous soup. For three days during the festival neighbors, co-workers, and relatives all come and share in a bowl of this specialty prepared food. By the third day, in places like in the rural areas where electricity and refrigeration are scarce, it is recommended that you stop visiting. At this point, the stew can begin to hold considerable amounts of bacteria and other vomit-inducing critters.

The stew and I never quite became friends.

"*Salem-ale-kum,*" we greeted the woman standing in front of me. She approached and kissed my friend and me on the cheek; her eyes were twinkling as she led us to her special guest room. We entered an elaborately decorated room with plush pillows, where gold sparkling curtains graced the wall that were bright purple, and accented with glitter. A Persian rug full of designs and deep colors covered the floor. The Afghan guest room is the most important room of the house, and much effort is taken to make it incredibly ornate.

The woman quickly returned carrying bowls of the sheep stew. I groaned. Had she brought any other treats, I would have politely refused the stew, but it is customary when the household itself has slaughtered an animal to only serve stew. Not wanting to offend her, I began eating slowly. I knew it was the third day of *Eid*, and as I started to eat the tepid broth, I dreaded what lay ahead.

Three o'clock in the morning, my eyes suddenly popped open. My stomach churned wildly. I bolted out the door, tripping over LEGOS as I tried to make my way toward the bathroom. As I retched into the squatty toilet, my desire for western plumbing increased with each heave. I spent the next several hours regretting having eaten the stew as my body shivered and pitched to rid itself of the food poisoning that came from ingesting it. It was a sacrifice indeed to have eaten it.

For Muslims, faith centers on honoring God enough so that He accepts them.

In the Jewish calendar, Rosh Hashanah is the celebration of the Jewish New Year.[12] It is the first day of a series of ten days considered the Days of Repentance. It is a time for looking inward and evaluating one's life and good deeds. Often on Rosh Hashanah a *shofar*, the ram's horn, is blown, it is possibly done as a call to repentance.

During this time, the story of Abraham binding his son is read.[13] When an angel appeared at the last moment, he provided a ram to take the place of Abraham's son, stopping Abraham from committing the ultimate sacrifice. According to Jewish tradition, God told Abraham that the ram's horn, the *shofar*, should be blown on Rosh Hashanah to commemorate the offering that God provided in the place of Abraham's son.

Why the need for a Day of Atonement? Atonement is a word that implies *something needs to be bought back or paid for.* Traditionally, this day that was first mentioned in the Book of Leviticus, was the day the high priest donned sacramental robes, entered the Holy of Holies, and sacrificed a bull for his sins and the sins of the priest's household. Then he took two goats and sacrificed the first to the Lord, and the other became the scapegoat, and would have the sins of the Israelites confessed over it. Then the goat would be released into the desert, representing that a way of escape had been found.

This was the day when God pardoned the wrongs that the nation of Israel had done against Him. On this day, the sacrificial gift of the blood of an unblemished animal was offered as atonement for their sin. For the Jewish faith, it was about confessing and appeasing God for the wrongs they had done as a nation.

The Christian faith actually doesn't have a specific day where they celebrate the account of Abraham being tested to give up his most beloved possession, the son born to him in his old age. That is because it's believed it foreshadows a greater story—the sacrifice of Jesus on the cross.

"Behold the Lamb of God that takes away the sins of the world!"

The passionate cry of John the Baptist reverberated off the surrounding hills, and fell upon the ears of the eager men and women who had gathered around to hear a message of change, and to be baptized as they vowed to change their own lives. When John spotted Jesus, drawing closer to the crowds of people that John had been baptizing, the words burst from his inner being, booming out words of hope: *The Messiah had come!*

For Christianity, it is about accepting that God has done something miraculous for us.

The ritual of animal sacrifice in the Bible was observed as reconciliation to God for the sins we have committed. Blood was shed in a ritual way for the sins of the nations or for individuals. Animal sacrifices were a temporary method, and represented a time to come.

Jesus' sacrifice was a one-time sacrifice that lasts forever. The act of believing is an act of releasing our past to God, uncovering the truth. It is an act of letting go, admitting we were wrong, and accepting that only Jesus atones for our sins. God has made a way for us to be forgiven and to forgive, and to live a life connected to him free from guilt.

* * *

When I was nineteen, I came upon Drew again in a grocery store. I'm not sure he recognized me, but if he did, I didn't give him a chance for an encounter. As the pain from all those years ago welled up, I briskly walked the other direction, and the feelings of hate overwhelmed me. I then realized I needed some healing, and I needed to forgive him. As I was later praying about it, God placed these words in my head. "Melissa, if someone at age eight treats others with such contempt, imagine what his home life must have been like."

I thought, "It's true." We learn hatred from others. Often the bully has something broken in them. I don't know if this was true for Drew, but I was able to forgive him, and that day I moved on. The beauty of the gospel is when we forgive and are forgiven, we are able to fully seek out the purpose that God has for us.

Chapter 10

Inmates Next Door, Morning Coffee, and Finding Freedom

Finding Our Purpose

In a day, thirty opium-smuggling inmates became my next-door neighbors. From a tiny window in my kitchen, I discovered I could see into their prison walls, and observe their world. And, so I did…

Thump, thump, thud. I heard a heavy knock on our metal gate. I was slow in opening it, and the pounding continued. After unlocking it, an Afghan policeman in an olive-drab uniform and coordinated square-brimmed baseball hat gave me a toothy grin. Then he sneered at me, looking me up and down, surprise registering on his face to find a foreign woman behind the door. He gestured to a pile of wooden poles and coiled razor wire lying beside him, and he said something to me. There was a word I couldn't comprehend, which seemed important to understand because he kept using it.

The policeman gestured again to the barbwire and wooden poles, and repeated that he wanted to enter the yard and install them on our far wall. I was sure our office hadn't ordered this much extra security measures.

"Wait. I have to make a phone call."

Irritated, he waited, because Mattie, our stranger-fearing dog, was loose, and her substantial frenzied barking persuaded him to listen to me.

I called our office, and the manager answered. I wasn't happy with what he had to tell me. "Jail! Are you serious?"

"Don't worry, they're only drug smugglers caught in Tajikistan and returned to the Afghan government. The government will hold them for one month, and then they will be released. It won't be a problem."

Opium and drug smuggling has been a problem for years in Afghanistan. Both the government and the military made a big show about the eradication of poppy fields, but the reality today is the growth and sales of opium has never been higher. In Badakhshan a section of the province has always grown opium, and the opium is smuggled by different criminal groups to Tajikistan or in the other direction, to Pakistan. The one-month sentence was given as an attempt to show that the government was punishing the offenders. Now they would be my new next-door neighbors.

The dog's barking brought me back to my current reality. Drug smugglers and opium...were his words meant to reassure me? I knew these were tough and most likely dangerous men. Realizing I had no choice, I chained up the dog, and in came the policemen bearing their wooden beams to extend the wall and erect the razor wire.

Later on, a well-dressed government official knocked on my gate and handed me a business card. He said, "If anyone escapes over your wall, call this number."

Seriously! I had a discussion with the neighbors and with my husband John. All of us were irate with the landlord for renting this property for a prison located smack in the middle of the city.

The first night, the generator of the prison ran continuously, and the extra lights glared into my bedroom window illuminating my fears and annoying my ears and my eyes. I slept sporadically, rose early, and stumbled into the kitchen. I glanced out the half-size window in the corner of our kitchen, and I realized I could see into their courtyard below.

I thought of the Van Gogh painting, *Prisoners' Round,* that he painted during his stay at an insane asylum. It is a haunting picture where the men, dressed in drab clothing, line up and march soullessly in a circular formation, as brick walls loom up, trapping them in on all sides. As you look at the picture, inevitably your eyes will focus on one man in the picture, since the picture is a copy of another artist. It can't be Van Gogh himself, but a person is drawn to this man and you can feel his despair, his aloneness. Did the original artist mean for it to represent all of us in some way or another— people who march a life path that's often dictated by others? We may feel trapped, unable to break free, marching endlessly in an unending circle.

It was breakfast time for the inmates. The din of glass plates and cups being ladled full with food reached my ears. They hid their shaved heads beneath under-sized stocking caps, as smoke whiffing from cigarettes lingered in the brisk February air, and about fifteen weathered-looking men in their blue-grey prison uniforms moved restlessly around the compact courtyard. One man taller than the rest, his freshly shaved pale scalp, with its jet-black stubble, stood in contrast to the rest, and when a policeman said something to him, he shifted out of sight. I studied the rest of their faces, thinking they had all once been little boys like Malcolm, and wondered what kind of life you have to lead to end up in a prison in northern Afghanistan.

Every morning, our routine repeated. I stumbled into the kitchen to make French-pressed coffee from freshly ground beans, a coveted treat in a world of tea drinkers, imported from a shop in Dubai.

As the water came to a boil in my whistling kettle, through the window I watched them line up as the meal was ladled into their glass dishes. Smokes followed, and then they wandered aimlessly around the dirt compound, interacting little, ever moving to keep the cold at bay.

Soon they disappeared until afternoon exercise.

The whole group gathered in the middle of the yard, behind a line etched in the dirt, a gigantic rock lay at their feet. The first inmate picked it up and his face strained under the pressure, veins popping, face flushed, he heaved it as far as possible. The spot it landed was marked, and a prison guard carted the rock back to the starting line where the next man hoisted it up, trying to best the man in front of him. Every afternoon it was repeated: the same game, the same strategies, and the same winners.

The man I noticed that first morning with the strikingly black stubble was bigger than the rest. He was the leader, the champion.

When it began to get warm, they removed their stocking caps, and warm shirts came off, revealing white muscle shirts beneath. That was all that changed. The monotony of their existence got to me, an outside observer, and I became disinterested and stopped watching.

I'm glad God never gets tired of me.

The period when the prisoners moved in next door was a particularly trying time for me, not just because I was afraid of having dangerous men living with only a courtyard wall between us, but because it was winter time in Faizabad. Being a mother of small children, I went through cycles of being busy working at different projects part-time and then periods of times when my only focus was the home and taking care of my children. As much as I loved my children, I wanted to make a difference in the community that I was living in, and I was frustrated when my schedule needed to revolve around my children's schedules, washing mounds of dirty laundry, bouts of sickness, and taking care of a home without all the modern conveniences like dishwashers, vacuum cleaners, and water heaters.

So Monday would turn into Tuesday, Tuesday into Wednesday, and Wednesday into Thursday, each day similar to the last…until it felt like a self-imposed prison. I had established routines of waking up, getting dressed, brewing my coffee, clicking through social media sites, cooking oatmeal for my kids, creating activities, reading story after story, cleaning the house, writing emails, answering random knocks at the gate, preparing and heating lunch and dinner, boiling water for bathing, dropping the children into bed, and being on alert for security incidences. After a long day I'd enter into half-hearted conversations with John, and then maybe watch a movie on the computer and drop exhausted into bed. In the morning, I opened my eyes only to start it all over again.

When I got in this cycle, my soul cried out for meaning and purpose, because I knew I was never meant to live purposelessly. I could easily feel like the prisoners shuffling aimlessly to and fro around a tiny yard.

When I recognized that I was in one of these moods of self-pity, believing the lie that I was living far away from family and friends for nothing, I knew I couldn't allow my circumstances to get the best of me. So at these times, I looked for opportunities to serve. Then it became a reality, and I got to teach at a preschool for my kids and others, and I loved it. Later, I become a trainer for a course that our organization was going to start teaching in the province of Badakhshan. As a nurse I knew about the high maternal death rate in Afghanistan, and I was very passionate about the Birth Life Saving Skills (BLiSS) project.

It was a community development course that focused on safe birthing practices, recognizing warning signs of pregnancy, and how to respond when emergencies arise. My favorite lesson started with a story titled, "The Road to Life and the Road to Death." I taught several lessons to the office staff who would later teach in more remote areas. Another winter I drew pictures for nutrition lessons that would be used in community development projects that focused on mothers feeding their babies properly. I also taught first aid classes to the office staff.

From the cloth BLiSS dolls used in the class to represent a newborn baby, I copied the pattern, and spent a snowy cold week or two teaching about eight neighborhood girls how to sew them. Then we transformed them into beautiful dolls with painted eyes and flowing clothing. From that project, months afterwards I was still finding bits of cotton in the carpet in the room where we worked. Many of those girls had never owned their own doll.

My house became a favorite place for the neighborhood kids to play. We colored, I went through a series of English lessons with them, and I sporadically taught English lessons to older teenage girls. I did art lessons with the other expatriate kids living in the area, and later I discovered I had a passion for writing. Sometimes, Mirjam watched my children, so I could visit some of the neighbors and take their blood pressures of those who had chronically high blood pressure, or I would take care of their simple health needs. I tried to be a blessing and let God's light and love shine through me. I can't say I always succeeded, but I was able to incorporate these tasks and projects into my and my children's daily lives. Most importantly, I no longer felt like my life was one monotonous drag.

* * *

I eventually stopped watching the inmates, although I kept peeking, and one day I noticed something different. The Afghan flag was taken down, the outside kitchen disassembled, and the prisoners were embracing and slapping each other vigorously on their backs and shaking hands with their wardens. Then they walked out the door. Once again the policeman came and knocked on my door. I chained our dog as the razor wire was disassembled. The empty lot bore no reminders of what it had been.

These prisoners were free. And it was a good reminder that so was I, when I look beyond myself, and chose to accept the grace and opportunity given to me by God. I invited Him to be a part of my everyday life long ago, but I realized I can miss out on opportunities when I focus too much on myself. This was true when I was in Afghanistan, and is also true today.

My mundane existence changes to being extraordinary when I seek Him—and when I align my life with God's, my routine is broken. My freedom can move me from observing inmates, to praying for them, to one day visiting them. My work can become my ministry when I befriend those around me, and my commute can become a time to pray for world issues. If I shut off the television, my computer, and my smart phone, and engage in people's lives nearest me, all around me vivid color and purpose spring up. When I embrace the liberty extended to me by God's grace, he gives me the courage to do what I never thought possible, in the small and the big things of life. I stop letting my circumstances stagnate me, and I listen to God's gentle voice nudging me to become involved in issues that He cares about.

By becoming involved in Afghanistan, I not only found my purpose, it freed me to continue to observe a culture that seemed more like the time that Jesus was on earth than the modern one in which I had grown up. Specifically, God took me through a time of examining the "I AM" statements that Jesus spoke about himself.

I AM the bread of life, I AM the good shepherd,
and I AM the light of the world.

Chapter 11

Tandoors and the Naan of Life

Jesus Our Nourisher

While shopping for bread in America, I push my cart to the bakery and briefly stare at the multitude of choices: rye bread, whole grain, honey wheat, French, Italian, and seven-grain. Then I buy the most nutritious loaf for the best value. The bread is brought home and made into toast or sandwiches. Little thought is given to how it is made—or what value it has in my daily life. I love bread in all shapes, sizes, and textures, but it really is a minuscule part of my life.

Afghanistan is a country that loves rice, but bread is their staple. Like in some places in India, it is called *naan*. It is served at every single meal. One day we had an Afghan friend over for pizza, and at the end of the meal, he asked, "It was very good, but where was the *naan*?"

Many traditional practices have been handed down for generations, including bread making, and it's a necessary one where poverty can be a constant foe. In our own neighborhood, we were able to watch this practice at our street corner bread shop.

The huge mud oven stood before me. I watched, fascinated, as the bare-handed man stuck the circular flat dough onto the sides of the blazing *tandoor*. After the flatbread had finished baking, he stuck a hot metal poker into the oven to easily dislodge the loaves one by one. The baker grabbed the loaves and threw them under a wool blanket in order to keep them warm as long as possible. I paid my twenty Afghanis (about forty cents) and popped two hot, crispy *naans* into my cloth bag designated for bread. The man behind me did the same, but he bought ten *naans*.

The bread is baked every day, through the heat of summer, the cold of winter, and the rains of spring.

Naan is found all over the country in different shapes and sizes. There are boat *naans,* which are oblong and thin; circular *naan*, with holes pricked all over them in fancy designs; and *naan-e-khonagee*, which are a huge circular naan made of coarsely ground wheat flour and baked at home. This is my personal favorite, and reminiscent of my time spent in a village in Badakhshan. There is two-dollar *naan*, which are stretched and pulled until they are at least six feet long, and bought for large families or parties. There is *naan* that is torn off and eaten with kabobs, and *naan* that is used as sandwich wraps.

All of these are not made in a factory, but are prepared by the hands of men and women who have learned the secret of making this sustenance. They are made by women who get up at three in the morning so the fresh bread can be ready to sell in the bazaar, where it is carted by their children in wheelbarrows, and sold along the side of the road for people's breakfasts. The men are considered the professional bakers, and they get up equally early and prepare the dough to bake and sell their naan at the street-corner *tandoors*.

Bread is the main staple that's eaten two to three times a day throughout Afghanistan, but in the remote communities, far from city centers and markets, people live the whole winter on *naan* and tea. That is all they have. The bread keeps them one step away from starvation. Give us today our daily bread.

Farmers throughout the country work hard to get their wheat crop in as soon as the melting snows will allow. Some areas of the country are fortunate; it is warm enough to get two crops in during the short growing season, and more wheat equals more bread. In the parts with high altitude, the snows melt long enough for only one crop. The farmers will trade or sell valuable animals later to obtain more of this precious commodity.

After the fall of the Taliban government in 2001, an incentive arose throughout the rural countryside—girls started enrolling in schools in substantial numbers. Various programs promised them that every month a bag of wheat would be given to the family for each girl who was in school. Women also began entering adult literacy courses and other skilled courses for the promise that at the end of the course, a bag of wheat was the prize. This was a worthwhile trade for a population that was usually encouraged to stay at home. Who could say "No" to a bag of wheat—wheat needed for making precious bread that keeps little stomachs full and old ones happy.

One day, embarrassment washed over me as I witnessed a girl enter my yard, pick up a leftover piece of *naan* that Mattie had left on the ground, kiss it, and place it high up on a window ledge. I realized that by leaving it on the ground in the dirt and dust, in her eyes we had been disrespectful to the *naan*. *Naan* is revered, with strict societal rules about throwing it out, how it should be carried, and stories that honor it. Even leftover bread is recycled. It gets rock hard after a day or two, so anything left is crushed into breadcrumbs and fed to chickens, cows, goats, or donkeys.

Coming back to America after an extended time of being away, I eventually went grocery shopping and found myself gawking at the excessive amount of food that I had long ago forgotten existed. The infinite choices overwhelmed me, and the aisles seem endless. My eyes glazed over as I tried to decide which type of peanut butter I should buy. Then my mind wandered back to a mudroom, where I sat on the floor around a table cloth laid out in front of me. Oily, farm-fresh eggs with sautéed tomatoes and onions and crisp *naan* on the side, were set in front of me. I savored every bite, since it was shared out of scarcity, not abundance. The gift of poverty is being able to relish the simple things in life.

Then there is Jesus. When Jesus walked on this earth, he used common, everyday objects to illustrate the truths he was trying to explain. Bread was one of them. In John 6:35, Jesus said to them, *"I am the bread of life; whoever comes to me shall not hunger, and whoever believes in me shall never thirst."* The people in Jesus' time also had bread as their main staple. They spent an enormous amount of time planting wheat to make bread. They watered it, prayed against drought, and harvested it, grinded it, and finally they baked it.

Having lived in a bread-based culture, I now understand what Jesus was referring to when he said, *"I am the bread of life."* I understand what He was saying. I am it; revolve your lives around me! I will nourish and take care of your deepest desires. I am the *naan* that brings life: the *naan* that you crave so much, work so hard to make, think about three times a day, and will not only keep you one step away from death and starvation but will cause you to thrive. I am your spiritual bread, feast and be full.

Next time you throw a loaf of bread wrapped nicely in plastic into your shopping cart, just remember your "Bread of Life!"[14]

Chapter 12

Our Taxi-Driving Shepherd

Jesus Our Guide

The lithe music danced and swirled through the open window. Looking out the window I saw the verdant green mountains with sharp metallic-colored rocks. The dotted specks of white, cream, and brown moved over the land, munching. High up in the mountains the shepherd sat, playing his eight-holed wooden flute, passing away the lonely day. It was spring in Afghanistan.

The winter snow had melted, the sierra-colored dry earth had soaked in the moisture, and the rainy season had begun. For three months, the surrounding foothills would be vibrant, bursting with new growth, red and purple wildflowers, and ideal conditions to plant wheat. After the rains ceased, the blazing sun would annihilate all vegetation, returning the foothill to their pre-rain stark-and-rocky existence.

In the spring, the shepherds guide the flocks of sheep and goats from their winter grounds to the higher pastures. During this time, every evening as I lay in bed, I could hear the din and bleating of large numbers of sheep and goats moving through town in the early morning light as the nomads began to migrate into the hills. They brought with them tents, their flocks, and an occasional cow and donkey to graze and grow fat from the passing wealth of the land. Lambs, kids, calves, and foals were born and joined their mothers in romping, skipping, and stumbling over the steep hillsides. There was much to celebrate!

I loved seeing the shepherds when I encountered them, their traditional *pakhtas* wrapped around their shoulders, with a long stick in their hands. They would march confidently alongside their flock. The sheep huddled and trotted together like one huge wooly mess as they were guided through busy bazaars and down the streets of the bustling cities.

One day, in the enormous city of Kabul, some shepherds tried to move their herd through the congested streets. Occasionally, a sheep would break loose to eat a tasty morsel of garbage on the side of the road. Chaos erupted as the sheep started bumping into each other as they all tried to follow the wayward trash-muncher. The shepherd, along with his apprentices who were several little boys in identical frocks, restored order in seconds, and the flock moved again, united in forward motion.

These were the good shepherds. They cared about their sheep, and they felt responsible for them. Jesus referred to himself as the good shepherd. The good shepherd was an illustration about how God is our guide.

The good shepherd directs the sheep to lush grass, he leads them to the fresh underground springs seeping out from crevices, and he protects them from stray dogs and dangerous cliffs.

The Bible is full of illustrations about the shepherd. The most beautiful and comforting is the one we have often heard read at the end of a loved one's long life.

> *The LORD is my shepherd; I shall not want.*
> *He makes me to lie down in green pastures. He leads me beside still waters.*
> *He restores my soul.*
> *He leads me in the paths of righteousness for his name's sake.*
> *Even though I walk through the valley of the shadow of death,*

I will fear no evil, for you are with me;
your rod and thy staff, they comfort me.
You prepare a table before me in the presence of my enemies;
you anoint my head with oil;
my cup overflows.
Surely goodness and mercy shall follow me all the days of my life,
and I shall dwell in the house of the LORD forever.
    —Psalm 23

Beside the good shepherd, in Afghan society, there was another guide that most of the time I was extremely grateful for: the taxi driver. The taxi driver in many ways reminded me of a modern-day shepherd, hustling and directing the flocks of humanity throughout the perils of modern-day cities.

The major cities in Afghanistan are over-run with a variety of taxis that swerve, speed, turn, stop, brake quickly, and deliver their patrons to a variety of posts. The taxis come in many shapes and sizes. Old rusty Soviet-style taxis rattle along the pothole-filled roads; others might be new sleek designs in silver, with air condition and loudspeakers. Some are station wagons or vans, and taxis decorated with neon lights and pulsating with sound from an added bass amplifier. Some might even be people's private cars, used for the day to make an extra buck.

For the nine years we lived there, we never owned a vehicle, which meant we took a lot of taxis. I have had my share of great taxi drivers, along with my share of those I felt like I should leap out at the next intersection, as soon as the taxi slowed down going around the roundabout.

Like the following story:

"Where would you like to go?" asked the wrinkled man in the beat-up taxi as he ground to a stop near the side of the road where I was standing in front of an eye hospital.

"I'm going across the city near the girl's high school. My home is near there. How much?"

The taxi driver paused and stared hard at me. "Two dollars." Relieved he didn't charge me an inflated foreigner price, I agreed and got in the back seat. We bumped along, hitting pothole after pothole.

"Is that a good eye hospital?" he asked.

"Yes, do you have eye problems?" I asked.

He squinted as I enquired and replied as we weaved in and out of traffic. "I used to drive a truck up and down the Salang Pass. The snow was so bright sometimes I would see flashes of light for days afterward. I have trouble seeing things close up and seeing things far away." He gestured with his hand.

I realized there was *no way* I should be in this taxi with a taxi driver who was both near-sighted and far-sighted!

"Yes, it is a really good eye hospital, you should go," I replied.

Praying the whole way home, I became acutely aware of the bikes, children, and other vehicles spinning around us. I sat on the edge of my seat, ready to point out anything we came across, hoping my driver also saw them.

I loved to ride with another taxi driver. He had the oldest and rustiest taxi that squeaked and rattled over the worn-out roads, but he would smile kindly at me, while nodding his head with his little white prayer cap perched on top. He never asked me inappropriate questions, and would always take me where I needed to go. I would tell him to head first to the small shop across town that sold imported goods. As we drove along, he would tell me about his family and life when the Russians controlled the city.

While I was in the shop getting everything I needed in imported goods, he patiently waited. Then I would tell him I needed some meat, but that I wanted really good meat. Again, we would head to another area of the city, and he helped me negotiate and haggle a fair price for the piece of meat I needed. The meat would be weighed out, and he would help me carry my purchases back to the car. Then we were off to the fruit bazaar, and we would go through the same process picking out lush peaches, oranges, and apricots. When all the shopping was done, my taxi guide told me about the city and his country as the rusty taxi creaked towards my home.

He would deposit me and all my goods at the door, help me unload my baby and my purchases. I would tip him generously. His price was never a high one, and he would politely say good-bye. He was the good taxi driver and a trustworthy guide.

The good taxi driver, like the good shepherd, is one that takes care of his passengers. The taxi driver will guide his passengers throughout the city on the best routes, with the least amount of trouble for them to arrive at their designated spot. The driver will know the terrain, and when and where it is best to travel. He will stay clear of known dangers, and he will continually scan the changing territory, dodging bikes, fruit-sellers, and stray dogs, school girls carrying their UNICEF backpacks, the man selling balloons, and armored vehicles, while chatting the whole time.

The good taxi driver or the taxi shepherd, if you will, senses the needs of the passengers and adjusts his attitude to fit the situation. Are the passengers traveling to the hospital with a sick baby? If yes, then he will be reserved while sharing his stories of his own sick children, and lamenting the high cost of medical bills. If the travelers are new to the city, he will shout out random facts of history at a rapid pace as milestones and landmarks flash by. If his passengers have political views opposite of his own, he will spout out his viewpoints in an endless rant, but wish you well as you exit his vehicle, and then inform you that he would be pleased to escort you again anywhere you need to go.

The taxi shepherd is indeed a good guide because he knows this is his responsibility. Like the shepherds in Jesus' time, the modern-day shepherds of Afghanistan continue to understand above all else, their responsibilities are to take care of the sheep. Jesus wants to comfort those he is speaking to— he wants to assure them he will never leave them nor reject them. He is the good shepherd, and he is our guide through the potholed streets of life.

When we have Jesus as our taxi-driving shepherd, we need to relax in the back seat, even when he takes us in a drastically different direction. We need to trust our shepherd when he says, "I know a better way."

One day I experienced this myself.

"Why are we going this way?" I grilled the taxi driver. "I want to go to the airport. I have never been on this road before." I probed, fearing the worst. If I was being kidnapped and taken in a different direction, I wanted the taxi driver to know I was acutely aware of his devious plans.

The old man with watery red eyes with bags underneath, kindly stared at me as he gripped the steering wheel and replied. "The road is closed through town, and I know a shortcut. I was born here; I have driven these streets for years. I will get you to the airport. I know the way."

The taxi-driving shepherd adjusts himself to whatever we are going through. He is able to bring comfort when comfort is needed, he can rejoice with us when celebration is called for, and he is able to bring hope to us when we are unable to see what lies ahead of us. He will never leave us, even when a pack of wolves or a violent demonstration lurks nearby.

When we stray away, like sheep have been known to do, he leaves the other sheep in a safe place, and goes in search of the one who has been diverted. He searches day and night knowing that the sheep must be found, or she will perish. Finally, he finds her, and it is a great celebration because every sheep is equally precious to the good shepherd.

The sheep know the good shepherd's voice and music; however, it sometimes gets confused about the troubles and philosophies of this world. Sometimes we seek out other places to get food and drink from, but it is hollow and false and leaves us malnourished spiritually. But, when we are allowing God to guide us, we know we are in the right place, in the flock of our Good Shepherd, Jesus, or in the backseat of our taxi-driving shepherd.

Chapter 13

Ancient Oil Lamps and Throngs of Cockroaches

Jesus Our Light

It was New Year's Eve 2007, and a celebration was underway at our house. Only we foreigners were crazy enough to welcome in the New Year during the dead of bleak wintertime. The rest of Afghanistan celebrates Nao Roz, their New Year, in mid-March, when spring is blooming. Midnight was swiftly approaching, and the old year was closing its weary eyes, quickly receding into history. My friend, Ingrid, suggested we go outside for the countdown, and cheer in the birth of the New Year. And, so we did. *10-9-8-7-6-5-4-3-2-1! Happy New Year everyone!* As we hailed in the New Year, the power was cut, and we found ourselves in total darkness.

The crisp January air seeped through our clothing, and our group of tired merrymakers shivered as we stumbled inside in the dark. I found some flashlights to help our guests gather up their belongings, which included blonde, curly-haired slumbering twin girls. After they left, John and I checked on Malcolm, who was sleeping in his crib, and then dropped into bed, not worried at all about the electricity. Power outages were frequent, especially in winter. If we had known we had just cheered in a month of blackness in the midst of the most brutal winter Central Asia had for years, we would have been a little less celebratory.

I have rarely experienced a moment of unwanted darkness in America. It is a country of 24-hour power with 24-hour lives. In the winter, night arrives at five every evening in Minnesota, but we know we can simply walk from room to room flipping on lights. We never think about what we would do if when we flipped a switch and nothing happened. Being masters of our own time clocks, we have never known anything different, unlike our ancestors whose lives revolved around the rising and setting of the sun. We live without thinking about the many places of the world that still struggle to push back the darkness.

When we moved to Afghanistan, electricity became elusive, like trying to catch a firefly in a glass jar on a midsummer evening. The light switches sometimes worked, magically illuminating everything. Other times, they remained stone dead and inactive. No matter how many times I tried the switch, nothing happened. When I needed the electricity the most, it would disappoint me. I would find myself in utter darkness, blind and desperate when I was in the middle of an extremely important task, like preparing a meal on a hot stove or changing a dirty diaper.

Some of the worst words in the world are, "Mom, I think I'm going to be sick!" These words became extremely alarming in the dark when you discover you can't turn on a light. It caused me to frantically grope around in a half-awake stupor, yelling at John to help me. Panicking as I tried to locate my flashlight, knowing I had only seconds before my child was going to vomit. All I wanted was to be able to see enough so I could keep him from retching on the bed.

In Afghanistan, I encountered multiple ways to make a ray of light. People use candles, flashlights, oil lanterns, gas lamps, generators, and even their cell phones when there is no electric power. Their single objective is the same as anywhere else in the world when it comes to night. They want to hold back the darkness so they can see, and so they can live. It is evident that as human beings, we were not created to be creatures of the dark. Cats, owls, and cockroaches seem perfectly suited for this task. But, without the help of some source of light, we are useless.

This obsession for humans can be observed throughout history. Afghanistan is an ancient civilization where archeologists continue to dig and find remnants of past lives. Some of these are displayed in the Kabul Museum.

During a visit to the museum, I noticed of all the oil lamps found at the digs, most were rustic shallow clay or bronze basins, where a wick would sit in a flammable liquid, most likely olive oil. I could picture them burning gently among a group of travelers who were sharing their tales as they consumed their evening meal. Others lamps were quite elaborate, like the double-headed cat-like lamp, with four golden legs. The wicks could be stuffed into the bronze lamp's cat's ears, and sit in the belly of the feline, slowly lapping up the oil, and brightening the way of a second or third century Silk Road tradesman.

No one is quite sure when man began to press olives and used the oil for a light, but we know it was from a very early period. In the Biblical world extending throughout the Mediterranean, olive oil was an invaluable commodity that would have been carried and traded along the Silk Road.[15] Imagine the discovery of juice that could be pressed out of a bitter fleshy fruit harvested from trees—and that this liquid could extend the length of day, and shine through the darkness.

> *You shall command the people of Israel that they bring to you pure beaten olive oil for the light that a lamp may regularly be set up to burn. In the tent of meeting, outside the veil that is before the testimony, Aaron and his sons shall tend it from evening to morning before the LORD. It shall be a statute forever to be observed throughout their generations by the people of Israel.*
> —Exodus 27:20-21

God wanted his temple and place of worship to shine throughout the whole night. This represented to the Israelites that God was their light, helping them to see through the dark. For centuries, humans have wanted to be masters of our own time, and we have fought against the impending blackness, like in the example of the oil lamp, because unless we were safely tucked into our beds, the darkness made us vulnerable. Darkness also caused us to stumble and stagger around.

One night, I needed to unplug a solar connection for our internet so it wouldn't drain the battery overnight. The citywide electricity had shut off around ten. I didn't have a flashlight with me, so I decided since the switch to shut off the solar power was right outside our bedroom door in the hallway, I would go out and feel along the wall until I found it. A minute later, I was screaming out in pain as my shin connected with something solid. Being unable to stop my momentum, I flew over what I later discovered was Emily's wooden chair left in the middle of the hallway.

As I lay on the floor writhing in pain, shivering in a pitch-black hallway, and trying not to be seriously upset at my daughter for leaving it there, it struck me that I had been pretty stupid to not bring a flashlight with me. I had thought the way was safe and clear, but the darkness had hidden the danger that lay in my path. Even a small ray of light—or a small clay lamp filled with the juice of an olive— would have helped me avoid the unseen obstacle.

Light protects us from tripping over objects misplaced by small children, but it also discourages great evils. For centuries, people feared the monsters, spirits, and creatures that lurked in the blackness, invisible until the sun waned...like cockroaches.

We lived in several houses in Afghanistan. All the houses have a large wall around them, and the yard is in the middle of the enclosed compound. Houses will either have an indoor or outdoor bathroom.

When we first moved to a city in the north, we stayed in a house owned by our office while we house-hunted for a place to live. We now referred to that house lovingly as the flea-and-cockroach house. It was supposed to be for only a few weeks, but we ended up living in it for almost five months. Our "favorite" feature of the house was its outhouse.

That first night when I opened the outhouse door, I almost fled from the compound for good. Turning on the overhead light, I saw hundreds of cockroaches climbing and scurrying over every inch of the squatty concrete commode. I screamed…and I'm not a screamer.

Because I had disturbed the cockroaches' all-night dance party, they were in a panic trying to get away from the bright glare. For a moment, I stood frozen in mortal terror, fighting my bladder's desperate urge for relief as I watched the scuttling insects.

I shut the door and called for John.

He assessed the situation and went at them with a flyswatter. Malcolm, age four, couldn't resist getting into the action, and grabbed a flyswatter, too. They destroyed the pests with the swatter flying right, left, up, down… smack, smack, squash—accompanied by a few giggles.

After thanking them, my feet cautiously crept over the carnage. I squatted, and all was well, until I reached for the toilet paper. As I picked up the roll, two roaches raced out, one proceeded up my arm. Again I screamed, dropped the toilet paper, deciding it wasn't needed, and promptly exited only to come face to face with the *chowkidor*.

In Afghanistan, it is common to have a groundskeeper or *chowkidor* on a property at all times, even if it has a small yard. They sleep in a small room near the gate. They do various odd jobs around the property, like gardening, taking care of chickens, chopping wood for heat in the winter, collecting water every morning, and going to the bazaar for grocery shopping. They also provide a measure of security, and even though they are unarmed, their presence is a deterrent for thieves.

Qaisim, the night *chowkidor*, who liked to sleep outside on a mat in the summertime, had witnessed the massacre and heard my scream. He tried to comfort me, while simultaneously laughing at me, "They're only roaches, don't worry."

"Hundreds." I could only shake my head and say, "Hundreds of them!"

It became John and Malcolm's nightly ritual to go cleanse the outhouse, with their swatters flying, and Malcolm began to look forward to this. There seemed to be an endless army to replace those killed the previous night.

I grew tired of not being able to use the outhouse as soon as it got dark, so I discovered a simple solution. I left the light on all the time, and then the cockroaches remained invisible. The power company shut off the city electricity at ten each night, so I never ventured out after that. Deep down I knew the roaches hadn't left; they were lurking there, waiting for the darkness, to emerge as creatures of the night.

Thankfully, light kept them at bay.

The idea of illuminating the world, of pushing back the darkness, is found not only in the Old Testament but continues into the New Testament. Jesus used this metaphor in the gospels to refer to himself, *"Again Jesus spoke to them, saying, "I am the light of the world. Whoever follows me will not walk in darkness, but will have the light of life."*—John 8:12

Light protects us from great harm; light holds back monsters and creatures lurking in the corners, and when there is deep darkness, the light shines out even brighter. *"The light shines in the darkness, and the darkness has not overcome it."* —John 1:5

God is a pure, warm, and guiding light for all to follow.

Chapter 14

Water in a Parched Land

Jesus Our Thirst-Quencher

The line of woman and children extended over a block down the street, and each one clutched several 10–15 liter plastic oil containers. These containers no longer held the precious golden liquid that is the staple of the Afghan diet. The oil jugs were empty, and my neighbors were waiting, in turn, to fill them to the brim with a far more precious commodity: drinking water.

As I passed the line, an elderly woman, whom I recognized as Amina, grabbed the empty water containers from the woman in front of her and hurled them into the middle of the street. Amina spewed a string of foul words as her long gray braids swung out in front of her. She blamed the woman of great evils, and cursed her. The accused woman hurled back insults that I couldn't quite understand, as the rest of the line inched closer, pushing the person in front of them, hoping to draw closer to the precious pipe spurting forth the life-giving liquid. I waited for the situation to turn into an outright brawl.

Cautiously, I approached the entrance to my home, which unfortunately happened to border the neighborhood water pipe. As I drew nearer to the elderly woman heaping curses on my neighbor for butting in line, she stopped mid-rant, and her weatherworn face melted into a very big smile. She kissed me on both cheeks, giving me the traditional greeting, and welcomed me home from my long trip. I returned the greeting and the kisses, and then disappeared behind the gate, not wanting to get trapped in the middle of a heated argument over water. I could still hear her continue her verbal onslaught.

Upon entering the gate, I groaned. I had just returned from a two-month vacation in America to a dried-up street and a Sahara-like yard. Earlier, the street we lived on was lined with ancient Plane trees. A Plane tree is native to Asia, and revered by Persians because its massive trunks and leafy branches provide a cooling shade to every foot-traveler.

However, in the name of progress, during those two months the charming lane was stripped bare by an iron beast, and now the hard-packed lane baked in the ruthless sun. Apparently, the digger had often broken the water pipe that brought fresh drinking water from a clean water source to our neighborhood. It had recently been fixed, thus all the neighbors were desperately clamoring to fill up their water containers.

This explained the edginess and bickering among my neighbors. Living without adequate water is the hardest thing I have ever done. Indeed, living without water accounts for much suffering around the world. I surveyed my yard again. The dry crumbling earth attested to this reality because it was completely void of life. Not one flower, a blade of grass, or one tiny tomato plant grew in my usually lush yard.

Being a mountainous country, with few major rivers, makes collecting water a daily issue. Many of the rivers are seasonal; the amount of water in the nourishing streams trickle down to only rocks and dust as the rainy seasons pass. A huge percentage of Afghans live without running water in their homes, not only in the rural areas but also in the cities. Bathing, washing clothes, cleaning your dishes, finding water for your animals, cleaning your house, taking care of your babies, watering your garden, and providing water for cooking and drinking are monumental tasks.

The job of filling up huge water containers and lugging them home falls to the children and the teenagers, or if there is no one else, the women of the family do it. Because Afghanistan is so mountainous, in the cities the houses have been built straight up the side of them. In many countries, these houses are prime real estate because of the incredible view and the coolness of the breeze in the summer. However, here those who dwell in the mountainside houses are in the grips of poverty, and have no water access. The families usually own a donkey they ride down the mountain with water containers heaped upon its back. The journey down is easy when the water containers are empty. But, these beasts of burden will then have to carry the heavy, water-filled containers back up the treacherous winding paths.

That summer continued to be a terrible time for water. Road construction was prevalent throughout the city, and the water pipe was turned on only twice a week for an hour in the morning and an hour in the evening. Tempers flared, and because we were the only foreigners living on our street, we were accused of and blamed for using too much water. It didn't matter that John and I were regularly contributing money for the pipe to be fixed. In truth, because we had indoor plumbing and a washing machine, we probably were using more water than anyone else, even though it seemed small in comparison to our normal usage in America.

The whole neighborhood was forced to gather water from the nearby river. The *chowkidor* carted the water from the river and dumped it into a tank in our yard. This was used only for bathing and washing clothes, and it was boiled when we washed our dishes. Our drinking water was filtered with a state-of-the-art system, but I worried about the long-term health effects. It turned out my fears were not unwarranted.

"My mom would like some medicine for worms," said our neighbor girl. "It's those big long ones. Every time she goes to the bathroom they are coming out."

My stomach lurched, but I realized this was a common occurrence here. She was telling me this because she was hoping we would have the medicine. I told her I would see what we could do. Roundworms are endemic in this country, but I knew that the summer water usage was contributing to this, because mainly it came from the river.

Like clockwork, every six months we took our deworming medicine. Later that day, the whole family was treated to an additional dosage of worm-be-gone. As the water shortage continued, my loathing grew for the rattling trucks and diggers that continued to work on our neighborhood road—and my desire to leave also grew.

Much of the world continues to live out their daily lives struggling to obtain the most precious natural resource to humans—water. During Jesus' day, it was the same. Each area had a central place to gather water. It wouldn't be a water pipe; it would have been a well. Fights would break out over the usage of a well, and when you really wanted to get back at your enemy, you filled up his well with dirt. This destroyed their ability to live in the area, to take care of their needs and their animal's water needs, so you were also destroying their livelihood. They would be forced to move on.

Perhaps the most famous story of Jesus' time dealing with water is with the Samaritan woman at the well found in John Chapter Four. It was noon as Jesus approaches a well, weary and thirsty from traveling. The well is now in Samaritan territory. He sat down and leaned against it. A woman, a Samaritan not a Jew, comes to the well to get water.

This woman from a different religion approached the well, and Jesus asked her for a drink. Jewish people did not eat nor drink with those not from their own religion. Jesus' culture was very traditional, as were the roles between men and women. We see this later when the disciples come to find him, and they cannot believe Jesus is speaking to a female.

The surprised woman pointed out Jesus' behavior to him, "How is it that you, a Jew, ask for a drink from me, a woman of Samaria?[16]"

Jesus replied, "If you knew the gift of God, and who it is that is saying to you, 'Give me a drink,' you would have asked him, and he would have given you living water.[17]"

She is taken aback. "Sir, you have nothing to draw water with, and the well is deep. Where do you get that living water?" Are you greater than our father Jacob? He gave us the well and drank from it himself, as did his sons and his livestock.[18]"

Jesus replied. "Everyone who drinks of this water will be thirsty again, but whoever drinks of the water that I will give him will never be thirsty again. The water that I will give him will become in him a spring of water welling up to eternal life.[19]" This sounds like a good deal, doesn't it? When your job is hauling water day after day in all kinds of conditions, the ability to never have to do it again would be a considerable gift.

The Samaritan woman replies:"Sir, give me this water, so that I will not be thirsty or have to come here to draw water.[20]"

Can't you hear the excitement in her voice as she dreams about never having to haul water from the well again—never having to trudge day after day from her home to the well and back again with that heavy container? The conversation continues and turns from him talking about physical needs to spiritual needs.

Jesus was not addressing her physical need for water, but her spiritual one. It is a need that we all have and feel at times; that relentless search for unfulfilled happiness or meaning for our lives.

Living without water is excruciating difficult. We learned this one horrible dry summer, it was life-sucking and draining daily work and it caused raw emotions to surface. Just like the human body cannot exist without water, our spiritual body can't live without God. Until, we let God connect with our spirit we will always be restless looking for ways to quench our thirst. What we need is exactly what Jesus offered the Samaritan woman at the well so long ago.

We can make peace with God by acknowledging that our wrong and hurtful actions have broken our relationship with Him, and accept that Jesus' death on the cross restored this relationship with our creator. Then the stopped well is opened up, the water pipe bursts with life-giving liquid, and our spirit is continually watered and refreshed by the Spirit of the living God.

Chapter 15

Silverbells, Blackbells, and a No-Name Rooster

An Introduction to the World of Hens and Roosters and the Mother Heart of God

Once, John found a kitten and brought it home, saying, "A Christmas cat for Malcolm." Despite the fact I am extremely allergic to them, I adore cats. I had a gross lapse in judgment for three days, before my watering eyes and itching temperament decided that we couldn't keep it. In the end, instead of a Christmas cat we ended up with a Christmas chicken.

Upon returning from finding the kitten a different place to live, John quietly shut the gate behind him. He took his long stride coming up our walk, but then he turned back.

Was he going to go back and get the kitten? I thought.

No, I saw someone at the gate. When I spotted the black hair and dark cloak of our evening guard carrying something under his arm, I wondered what it was.

It turned out to be a dark-brown dappled chicken about four months old. The date was December 23, and in honor of the time of year, our son christened the young chicken, Silverbells. And it was the beginning of our lives as chicken keepers.

Silverbells quickly became Malcolm's best friend. Malcolm followed her around the yard, and at first cautiously approached her. He gently grasped her and lifted her onto his lap, stroking her the whole time until she relaxed. He transferred all his desires for a pet to love onto this feathered fowl. Malcolm had a small leash that he would use to walk the chicken around the yard, and Silverbells hopped around behind him, contently trusting him and relishing his affectionate four-year-old love.

Silverbells became our treasured chicken, but she did seem lonely when Malcolm wasn't around. Summer approached, and I decided it would be a great experience for Malcolm and Emily to have baby chicks. I spoke with our day *chowkidor*, Aziz, and asked him if he could find a small rooster. I emphasized *khord* (small), knowing that roosters can be quite nasty. On a whim, I mentioned if he could find one, we would like another laying hen.

Two days later, I heard a torrent of squawking, and ran to look out my upstairs kitchen window to find the source of the hideous noise. Aziz had under his arm an upside down squawking beast, the biggest rooster ever seen. Another black hen's legs protruded from underneath his other arm. He let the protesting rooster drop, and a considerable display of green-tinted black feathers flared out, his dark red body glistened in the sun, and the golden glow of his neck shimmered. He was beautiful, but huge! The rooster, protesting his recent embarrassment, ran around the yard heinously crowing and cackling.

Upon going outside to meet our newest arrivals, Aziz grinned at me. "Isn't he beautiful?" The rooster strutted in front of me, and as I took in his immense size I wondered how "small" could ever be applied to this beast.

Laughing, I recalled going to a meeting with a bunch of women, and instantly being able to guess which shoes belonged to Aziz's wife by how ornate and fancy they were. He had an eye for beauty. He must have stumbled upon this gorgeous subspecies of the Red Jungle fowl, and my instructions about it being small simply slipped his mind.

The hen was a dingy midnight black with molting feathers and a naked fleshy neck. She looked tired and worn, and more ready for the frying pan than for laying eggs. *Maybe they had just thrown in this old bird with the purchase of the rooster?* I thought.

The rooster continued to crow, and I let Mattie off her chain. She had never bothered with Silverbells, but I was unsure about the rooster. When I let her go, she took after the rooster full throttle as he spirited around the yard as if his life depended upon it, always managing to keep one step ahead of the dog's gnashing teeth. Mattie didn't appear to really want to catch the rooster, just to put him in his place.

The hen was named Blackbells, and though we tossed around several names for the rooster, none of them ever did stick, perhaps because of his aggressive nature, he just became the no-name rooster. The rooster had a particular hatred for our downstairs neighbor and co-worker. Whenever she entered the yard or when she would get near him, he would charge her at full speed.

Blackbells and the rooster were harder for Malcolm to love, not having been raised as pets. Never having raised multiple chickens before, I soon discovered that my introduction of "friends" for Silverbells had reduced her to the bottom of a very real pecking order. It was high-school cliques and domination in the chicken coop.

Silverbells, being the youngest, now ate last. If she tried to eat first, she was chased far away by the rooster's brash scolding. Evidently, perhaps because Blackbells was older, she was his favored wife. He protected her from our dog, Mattie, and he always let her eat with him, but this didn't stop him from taking his just desserts with Silverbells. The first time he jumped upon her back, and she let out a startled squawk, I wanted to run out and push him off her. Didn't he know she was just a young chicken, how dare he molest her!

But, I realized the objective was baby chicks. Since I didn't know anything about when chickens were ready to sit on their eggs, I asked Ahmad. A chicken lays an egg either every day or every other day, but there are only a few periods in the year when they will actually brood/sit on them. When I asked Aziz about recognizing the signs of a maternal chicken, he made a clacking noise, raised his arms, and said, "When they start to make this noise, and strut around like this, you'll know." It seemed so funny, I wanted a second opinion, so I asked the neighbors, and laughed heartily when several of the women also lifted their arms, and started to make a deep throated clucking sound imitating a broody bird.

I didn't trust my own ability to recognize the clucking noise and activity that my neighbors had demonstrated, so Aziz was asked to keep me informed when he suspected the hens were ready to sit on their eggs. Finally, Blackbells showed signs that she was ready.

When I formulated the baby chick plan, I had hoped Silverbells would be the mother, but realized with her at the bottom of the pecking order, the task would fall to the older, experienced matron. Aziz daily gathered the eggs from the nest Silverbells and Blackbells shared, until he had fifteen eggs. Then they were placed all together into one nest. Blackbells instinctively fluffed out her feathers to gather in as much air as she could, until she doubled her size. She made it clear to Silverbells she was the mama.

Then she sat. And she sat. And sat some more. I worried that Blackbells wasn't getting enough food or water in the relentless heat of mid-July. I started to toss feed nearer to where she was sitting. I watched in fascination whenever she attempted to take a break and walk around the yard, the no-name rooster would make that same scolding, clucking noise that he used with Silverbells when she would try to eat first, and he would chase, yes, chase Blackbells back onto her eggs.

It was apparent the rooster had a father role in the raising of chicks. I assumed he just sowed his seed, and went on strutting and crowing. He seemed actively interested in at least making sure that a warm temperature was maintained for his chicks' survival. They were a family. This is something you miss with modern-day incubators.

My son and two-year-old daughter, Emily, had marked off twenty-one days incubation time on the calendar. When the twenty-first morning finally arrived, we eagerly ran outside expecting baby chicks. This is what happens when one is raised in a city. Disappointed when we didn't see any, we quickly realized that these things take time. However, the next day we could see one little beak poking out from underneath Blackbells' fluffed-up feathers.

I wanted to poke Blackbells off those eggs so we could watch the birth of the little chicks. But, Blackbells needed to remain, feathers fluffed up, keeping the eggs the perfect temperature to support life. Also, the rooster lurked in the background, ready to protect his offspring from the vicious dog and any other imaginary enemies.

For much of the day, we could see Blackbells shift uncomfortably and tuck her head under her wing to see how things were progressing. Little peeps reached our ears, and to our delight, we'd spot an occasional yellow or black head pop out from underneath the mother. Blackbells would quickly scoot it back under her wing, and out another head would pop, this time a dusty black one from the other side.

The next day it appeared that all of them had hatched. Eight little soft downy bundles with wiry feet could be seen peeking out, and each time Blackbells fluffed her feathers, and with a wing swiftly tucked them underneath her. She, like most mothers, wasn't quite ready for letting her newborn babes out into the world to face the big bad dog.

After two days, it became clear that even if Blackbells wanted to, she wasn't able to keep all these roly-poly bundles underneath her any longer. They had begun to eat the ground chicken feed that we had prepared for them, and they could squeeze out of the hen house any moment. Mattie was put on her leash, and then the door was opened for the rest that hadn't already found the portal to the outside world.

Blackbells promptly strutted out, and with the proud daddy rooster standing guard, she marched them around the yard. They lined up properly and followed behind her. She stopped, scratched in the dirt with one leg, and the line scattered and huddled around her. They cocked their little heads up, and you could almost see their brains working. "What is it, Mom? What did you find?"

She pulled up a grub, and they feasted. Now the eight all scratched away with her, realizing this movement was for a purpose. I never grew tired of watching these new lives stumble around, trying to keep up with their mother. When she entered the hen house, they all followed suit, and once again she fluffed up those dusty black feathers, and they would all gather in, safe and secure from any harm.

How many times have I felt like God doesn't care about my hurts? Or how many times have I even blamed Him for them—it's more times than I can count. Through watching our roly-poly, fluffy bundles be comforted by Blackbells, a verse in the Bible took on a whole new meaning. Jesus said when he was in Jerusalem and a group of Pharisees came to him and warned him that Herod wanted to kill him:

> O Jerusalem, Jerusalem, the city that kills the prophets and stones those who sent to it. How often would I have gathered your children together as a hen gathers her brood under her wings, and you were not willing! —Luke 13:34

And Jesus' profound statement...*and you were not willing* makes me realize that there were many times I thought I could do something without Jesus's help. And, I admit it has been true: I was not willing to accept His help, or I had felt like it was too late to ask for help.

How many times have I missed Jesus's comforting hand, his arm that he wanted to extend around my shoulder and let me know that He was there with me—like when I have heard the news of a dying grandparent, a friend battling through cancer, or I have just lost my job. He doesn't promise that we won't have pain in this world, but He does promise to be with us, to support us.

I have come to realize that to find and receive solace from God, I need to be willing to crawl under His wing, to let Him fluff his feathers over me, to sit close to Him, and allow Him to comfort me. God has many ways of bringing us comfort, and sometimes it is also from those who God brings into our paths like those in our messy-beautiful families.

Chapter 16

My Messy-Beautiful Worldwide Family
Community: The Heartbeat of God

In the beginning, God created the heavens and the earth. Something was formed out of nothing. The emptiness was filled with everything. Beauty, form, wind, light, water, animals, movement, color, and noise began. Life breathed in all its fullness and all its complexity and newness.

What a story it has been. Civilization upon civilization has fallen, sometimes literally, one ancient city being found beneath another one. Still time plods on, and trees grow from saplings, only to age and stretch out their arms, reaching out to the sky to brush the clouds. We enter into this world individually, small, helpless, and dependent upon others.

As we grow, we are a part of a network of people, a family. Our families come in various shapes and sizes. They are diverse cultures and of different ethnic groups, with different people playing out crucial roles that form us in our early years. The fact remains the same. We are all connected to some sort of family unit.

Sometimes we can exist within a network of members of this family, and still feel utterly alone—or somewhere along the way we have lost our family, through misunderstandings, through tragic accident, and through unforgiving hearts.

It was never meant to be this way.

Part of knowing God is realizing we have entered into a relationship with our creator who cares and is involved in our lives. God has multiple children, and when we become part of His family, we are adopted into one humongous messy worldwide family. When we moved overseas, discovering this worldwide family was one of our greatest joys.

* * *

"Would you like to go to the cloth bazaar with me? There is one not too far from here." Mirjam asked me with her German accent.

"Sure," I replied, not quite knowing what I was getting myself into.

At that time, Mirjam's daughter was ten or eleven months old, and Malcolm was only three or four months old.

We each had a stroller that we pushed down the streets of Kabul. In those days, strollers were rarely seen, and two foreigner women with their babies got a lot of stares and attention. After a little while, Mirjam turned down a muddy side street. I glanced at the large wheels on Mirjam's stroller, realizing that I had made a mistake. John and I should have brought a jogging stroller to Afghanistan, not one designed for American sidewalks.

Mirjam and I pushed and slid through the mud and shared our stories of why we had come to Afghanistan. She and her husband had moved there only six months before us. We made it to the cloth bazaar where I appreciated her grasp of the local language as we haggled for better prices on the fabric we were purchasing for clothes and sheets to be made.

This was the beginning of a very special friendship. Over the years, Mirjam, her husband, and what would become their three children, became some of our best friends, along with many others from Afghanistan and other parts of the world like England, South Africa, Australia, New Zealand, Scotland, South Korea, Canada, Finland, and Germany, to name a few.

By saying goodbye to our relatives and support network back home, we entered into an international community that became one large extended blended family—an international community who loved God and wanted to serve Him with all they had. It was one gigantic family tree that extended its far-reaching branches globally.

And, we were loved by so many in the national community. So many Afghans opened their homes to us, served us tea and their national dishes, endured our poor language abilities, and put up with us misunderstanding their culture.

Now that I have left Afghanistan, it is the friendships that I remember the most, and their absence that I feel the deepest. It is the moments of eating around large tables of simple meals of rice and beans, being invited for a neighborhood celebration, like when the grandchild comes to their grandparents' house for the first time, and all the neighborhood women gather together and eat until everyone's stomachs are about to burst. It is the visit accompanied with small gifts that I miss, like when my daughter Emily had broken her leg. It is the smiles, the neighborhood boy, Farwad, with his jet-black hair and winsome grin, who loved wearing Malcolm's superman cape, and raiding our cupboards for snacks that I will always remember.

Being part of this worldwide family meant being introduced to foods like the favorite Afghan rice and raisin dish, *Quabili Pilau,* and *Mantu* (my favorite Afghan dish,) a noodle dumpling stuffed with ground lamb; duck pate and salty licorice loved by the Finnish; *Haggis,* a Scottish dish made of sheep's heart, liver, and oatmeal and, if eaten correctly, is accompanied with a shot of whiskey; reindeer; *Banoffee pie,* a caramel and banana pie topped with whipped cream originating from England; German sausages; *Lebkuchen,* a gingerbread Christmas cookie; and South African *rusks,* a breakfast bar, shaped like a biscotti, eaten best dunked in one's morning coffee. As my palate expanded, so did my experiences and my friendships.

We had Christmas celebrations with families who were thousands of miles away from their own mother, father, sisters, brothers, aunts, and uncles, and at times, their wives or children. We shared cups of coffee as we shared our hearts about the struggles of living in a tea-drinking world that at times was so difficult to understand.

Together we learned how to love one another with our differences and we learned how to do this in community. I also learned so much about relationships from Afghan culture. Afghanistan is a relational culture. It is a culture that has time. People are more important than your job, goals, success, and what can be accomplished.

Afghan families are rich, diverse, and messy-beautiful. They are huge extended networks of cousins, aunts, uncles, nephews, nieces, half-sisters and half-brothers, grandpas and grandmas. There are strict social rules about honoring your family, and your identity is found not just in what you do, but who your family is. It is a wonderful experience to meet and enter into one of these families.

Opposite of this though, at times Afghan families like any American family, can be extremely controlling, and individuals are sometimes left with little personal choice. However, this is not the type of family God wants us to be a part of. He wants us to have the messy beautiful one. He wants us to be in loving, dynamic relationships where we are caring for others, and able to receive care and friendship from them.

This is what a church family is supposed to be. It is a global and diverse group of people, interacting, and walking with you through the everydayness of life. The messy beautiful family is there to celebrate the birthdays, the births, the graduations, the weekends, the weekdays, and to be by your side through the divorces, the separations, the miscarriages, the loneliness, the heartbreaks, the deaths, as well as the accomplishments of your life.

Our family should walk with us, reflecting God's promises and wholeness back to us, helping us believe the sun will shine again, and through the confusion, hope will resound. This family should call us to see God in a different and new way, or help us to part the dark clouds and remind us of his goodness when all we can say is, "This isn't working out like I expected."

At times, our extended Christian family will fail and disappoint us because, like our crazy mixed-up human families, they are not perfect. Yet, they are essential to our daily well-being and walking out our faith in a community. To find such a family, you don't have to sell all you own and pack it into three totes, but you do have to enter the door of a church or a fellowship to find others who are seeking after truth and love.

John, one of Jesus' disciples, put it plainly:

Beloved, if God so loved us, we also ought to love one another.

   —1 John 4:11

We need to be ready to say, "Let's go get a cup of coffee. Or why don't you come over and watch the game?" It is a step in the right direction to be able to connect first in community and later in spiritual matters. Living and interacting in this messy-beautiful community is the essence...the heartbeat of God.

As we learn to love and live in community from our messy-beautiful families, God will sometimes bring relationships into our lives that challenge us to learn how to love even more—for me one of these relationships was with a girl named Bahar.

Chapter 17

Befriending Bahar

God's Heart for the Disadvantaged

Bahar entered our lives accidently, and consequently, I learned an incredible lesson in love. One day, John stepped outside our gate and encountered a little girl wearing a white head covering and school-girl jacket. She was clutching a silver platter, and crying over dirt-streaked fried pastries that had fallen onto the ground.

Bahar, a girl of maybe nine or ten, had come to the school to sell her pastries and make some money for her family before she attended her third-grade classes. John immediately bought them all, and this marked the beginning of a several-year relationship with Bahar, a child of poverty. It's interesting to note that in Afghanistan they don't keep track of birthdays, and a child starts first grade when she starts losing teeth. I am guessing at Bahar's age because with her severe malnutrition, she looked nine, but could have even been ten or eleven.

This relationship became an on-going trial to me as I struggled to show her compassion and love her as Christ would. Almost every day she appeared at our gate, asking for bread, for money, and for scraps of paper that they could use in the fire, desperation clearly showing on her face. The bread and bits of food were easy to give. The scraps of paper and the cardboard boxes were even easier. It was the lies that were the hardest to take, and the persistent feeling that though she was desperately needy, she wasn't always telling me the truth about her situation.

Bahar usually walked around with a dirty pair of slippers on her feet that were broken and completely useless as shoes. One day she came to the gate. Pointing to her feet she said, "*Khola jan* (Auntie, dear) I have no shoes, could you give me some?"

I didn't have any her size in our house, so I gave her the three dollars that she would need for a new pair.

"This isn't enough. This will only buy the pairs that smell," she said, indicating she didn't want a cheap pair.

Apparently, in our house we purchased the plastic that smelled, because I never spent more than $3 on a pair of slip-on sandals. I thought, *Anything is better than what you are wearing. Where is my thank you?* I assured her that for her age and size, this was enough money.

I didn't see her for a couple of days. When I saw her again, she was still wearing the old sandals. I asked her if she had bought the new sandals yet. She shrugged and said it wasn't enough money, and began to plead for more money. I thought that maybe her mother took the money.

Then one day, one of our co-workers got a package from America with some clothes to distribute to those in need. In the box was a pair of really nice sneakers just her size. Elated that they were the perfect size, I gave them to Bahar. I saw her wear them to school twice, but then they disappeared, and she began asking for money for shoes again. I found out she asked almost all the foreigners in our neighborhood for shoes, which made me angry. I felt like I had been kind, and then discovered she had been lying to me. My anger increased when I went out to buy bread, and saw her walking down the street in nice clean shoes.

I realized that the shoe angle probably worked for her, and she likely was given more money when people saw her broken slippers. I reminded myself she was just a child, and she probably didn't want to beg.

So what if she was running a shoe scam and lying to me, how should I respond? What if that was me? What if she was my daughter? These thoughts ran through my head. Compassion flooded back in—but I stopped giving her money for shoes.

I could help out in other ways. First I found out where she lived. Bahar's home was situated on one of the mountains that surrounded the city where we were living. The homes there had no water, no electricity, and no trees. The mud houses were one or two rooms, and life was tough. It had a lovely view of the city, but was an incredibly difficult place to live. The fact that she trekked down the side of the mountain every day in the spring, winter, and fall to beg was quite a feat in itself.

One day I heard her knock at the door. "Do you want to buy some eggs?" "Yes!"

Ecstatic at the opportunity to contribute to her family's income, and not just have to give handouts, I purchased a dozen eggs. They were great! We loved eggs, and in a place where meat was hard to buy and to store, eggs gave us protein in our diet. Although we had our own chickens, they could never lay enough for our egg consumption. I told her I would buy some more if she was selling them again.

The next day she showed up with a dozen more eggs. I really didn't need another dozen, but I bought six more just to encourage her. When I went to use them later, I discovered every single egg was rotten.

The next day when she showed up at my door, I chewed her out. "Don't you ever bring me rotten eggs again! I won't give you a single thing, and I will never buy any more eggs again if they are rotten." I finished my tirade, and looked her in the eyes. I had the feeling she was used to being yelled at.

"Do you still want to buy the eggs I brought today?" Bahar asked.

"No," I replied, still steamed about the rotten eggs. "Come back tomorrow with good eggs and I will buy some." She did, but first I tested them in water to see if they were good before I gave her the money. This continued for about two months. I would buy eggs every other day from Bahar. Then one day she showed up with a quart of milk.

"What happened to the eggs, Bahar?"

"We had to sell our chickens. But, I have this fresh milk. You can buy a quart for a dollar."

I relished the thought of having fresh milk, since usually we only had powdered milk, or UHT milk that was radiated for long shelf life and didn't need to be refrigerated. It came from Pakistan, and to this day I am still a bit suspicious as to its health value.

I took the milk inside, and sniffed. It had a really strong odor, and it was still warm. I brought it to a boil on the stove knowing that it wouldn't be pasteurized, and then I let it cool. It had an earthy odor, and I was beginning to doubt that it was cow's milk.

Was it goat's milk? Malcolm and Emily wouldn't drink it, and neither would John. It made my coffee taste nasty. I decided to bake with it, and yet the flavor and taste permeated my baked goods.

I continued to buy the milk every other day, but it went straight down the drain. The idea was to support Bahar and her efforts to actually sell something, instead of just beg. Eventually, the cow was sold and the milk stopped coming along with the eggs. Bahar's begging continued, and my ability to love her waxed and waned as her lies increased.

She came to me requesting a school uniform, so I helped her. She never wore it. Later in a conversation with a friend, I found out she had also given Bahar money for a school uniform. I felt like a chump, but here was this very real girl who would show up at my gate. No one in her family had a job, and in Afghanistan, there is no welfare system, no government aide.

The question persisted: How were we going to help her? How could we help stop this cycle of poverty?

Finally, I suggested that she have her father come to our office so we could interview him for a job, to work as one of our guards. This had worked for a friend of ours who had twin girls come and beg at their gate every morning. There was an entry-level job at their office, and they had suggested to the girls to have their father come to the office to interview for the job. He came, was hired, and this ended the pattern of begging for this family. Maybe, it would work for Bahar's family.

Bahar had already told me that her father was dead; however, at another time she slipped and told me her father had gone to Iran and that she hadn't seen him in years. We suspected this wasn't true. When I suggested the job to her, a man claiming to be her father showed up at the office. Unfortunately, he had no references, and no one who could vouch for his character. Our Afghan office manager insisted he couldn't be hired.

The cycle of begging continued, and a solution evaded us.

The Bible is a book that honors the poor. We know an Afghan woman who decided to read the Bible. After reading it, her first comment was, "It says so much about poor people."

Indeed it does.

> *When the poor and needy seek water, and there is none, and their tongue is parched with thirst, I the LORD will answer them; I the God of Israel will not forsake them. I will open rivers on the bare heights, and fountains in the midst of the valleys. I will make the wilderness a pool of water, and the dry land springs of water.*
> —Isaiah 41:17-18

From the very moment I stepped onto Afghan soil, I began to encounter the reality of poverty and those whose lives are defined by it. At the baggage terminal, desperate men grasping luggage trolleys clawed at our baggage and heaved it onto their rickety carts before anyone else can haul it out to our vehicle just to earn a dollar or two to bring home to feed hungry stomachs. Then stepping outside the airport, taxi drivers hungrily bombard my husband and me with propositions to take us anywhere in the city.

The dust of the city blew in our faces, and as we drove through the streets we encountered a combination of modern office buildings standing next to bombed-out ones. The street vendors and beggar children selling packets of gum and one-cent balloons assaulted our vehicle as it crawled through the congested traffic. Desperate people were trying to exist, living barely one step ahead of the grave.

It is a mountainous and landlocked country with poor soil, few national products, and few industries. Though rich in natural resources like copper, they have never been used for their own people's gain. It is a land that has had much wealth pass over it throughout its long history from the days of the Silk Road, but the percentage of people who have benefitted from this wealth has been minuscule. It is a nation of people who are living buried six feet under the poverty line.

After living in a culture where the Afghan people suffer daily, I can better understand the face of poverty, especially, when I looked at it through Bahar's eyes. Compared to Bahar, my children had everything. They never went hungry, they lived in a house with more than two rooms with indoor plumbing, they never went cold due to lack of fuel for heat, they never had to sell things or beg for money, and they had books, dolls, bicycles, swings and money for sweets. In Bahar's eyes, they lived like royalty.

Birth control is viewed with suspicion, and the children brought into the world in this mountainous land do not have the same opportunities given to them that many do in Western countries. We may believe that we have gotten where we are by our own hard work and ingenuity, but much of our own success is due to the opportunities present from the school systems, economy, and health services that exist for us.

I would ask myself, "If I were born into Bahar's family, where would I be?"

The answer horrified me.

What is in God's heart when it comes to the poor—and what is our responsibility? As we read through scripture, we see a constant message of restoration, a message of lifting those in poverty both physically and spiritually from the situations that they are in, and treating people in these situations with dignity.

Many of the programs provided by the aid and development organization we worked for dealt with helping the poor and the marginalized break the cycle of poverty. There were literacy and computer lessons for women and men who never had the opportunity to go to school, and small-scale business courses for women who had minimal skills. Hydro-power projects were implemented that brought electricity to some of the remotest areas of Afghanistan, allowing children to study by electric lights instead of the dim oil lamps, as well as allowing women to spin their yarn late into the evening to make extra income for their families. Other projects taught women and men about safe pregnancies and how to prepare for the birth of a child, and how to recognize early signs of distress in labor so children would not be left motherless due to poor health care.

I loved these projects because they were impacting many. They made me hopeful. Yet, I was still faced with the reality of those living in poverty that I met on the street and Bahar at my door. With Bahar and the other desperately poor people I encountered, I struggled with their aggression— and with my response. Simply put, I wished they would go away. My one desire was to be able to walk down the street unharassed, and spend a day in my house without a knock on the door.

In many ways, I wished they would go away, because it was inconvenient and a stress for me.

Did God ever feel this way? I wondered.

In scripture, when Jesus was confronted with the masses who were desperate for his healing touch, he had compassion, not pity for them. I found out that he went away by himself, to recharge, to pray, but then he always returned to help those in desperate circumstances. My prayers changed because in my humanness and my selfishness I could not love enough. I would pray: Give me your sympathy and your compassion for Bahar and those in need, like you do for me, God.

I became tired of Bahar's begging, but God never did.

> *He raises the poor from the dust; and lifts the needy from the ash heap, to make them sit with princes, with the princes of his people.*
> —Psalm 113:7-8

When we seek God's will, when we pray dangerous prayers of, "God use me," we should not be surprised when a small girl wearing ripped sandals and holding a plastic sack of trash knocks on our door pleading with us for a pair of shoes—and may we, who have an abundance of resources, respond as Jesus would with love and wisdom.

Chapter 18

The Silent Whisper

God's Heart for Justice

The destruction of the twin towers in New York City on September 11, 2001, caused a series of events that toppled a brutal government in Afghanistan, after Western military entered Afghanistan to retaliate against the Taliban. Before that time, in some parts of the country, women were literally prisoners in their own homes, bound by unjust law. They were not free to go to the market, go to school, or to leave their houses without being fully covered from head to toe. With all the Western aid pouring into Afghanistan, those foreign governments point to the benefits and freedoms the Afghan women now possess. However, although they have been legally released from their housebound imprisonment, many women continue to exist under another type of captivity—an ancient culture with ancient rules.

Reading passages of the scriptures, I realized women faced many similar challenges as recorded in the Bible. Women in Biblical times also suffered from religious oppression based on rigid interpretations of scripture.

Jesus challenged this worldview when he walked on this earth, breaking the society rules and customs that he had grown up with by how he interacted with women. He treated them like intelligent beings, and as equals.

But the images that the media has repeatedly portrayed of Afghan women are only one face of the truth. When I looked beyond the veil, when the full burqa was raised, and upon entering their courtyards and their homes, I began to see them in a different way. Jesus tells a story that I think reflects their hearts more than the gruesome broken-down images that are often portrayed.

It is the story of the widow's offering:

One day when Jesus was at the temple, he looks up and notices all the rich people putting in their offerings. Then a widow comes forward and puts in two small copper coins; a pittance in the world of finances. And Jesus makes a statement here: *"Truly, I tell you, this poor widow has put in more than all of them. For they all contributed out of their abundance, but she out of her poverty put in all she had to live on."* —Luke 21:1-4

After the days of the Taliban rule ended, money poured into the country from all over the world as countries pledged and gave out of their abundance to help rebuild Afghanistan's infrastructure. Many of the Afghan women I met had hope for their nation, and many were trying to obtain skills, like literacy, business, and college degrees. Their goals were to better themselves, their families, and their nation. Many of them had only as much as the widow in this story. They had little to give, but they gave themselves. In the end, it will not be the outside funding that makes the greatest changes in this society, but the collectiveness of these women and their copper coins.

Before we moved to Afghanistan, God had led us to one particular scripture passage. It became the heartbeat of why we chose to undertake such a difficult task.

Isaiah 58 became our motivation. In this particular chapter, Isaiah the prophet is reprimanding the people who outwardly are acting religious by fasting. As they go through the motions of being religious, they are committing terrible injustices. Isaiah goes on to explain where our hearts and deeds should be focused as people of God:

Is not this the kind of fasting I have chosen: to loose the chains of injustice and untie the cords of the yoke, to set the oppressed free and break every yoke?

Is it not to share your food with the hungry and to provide the poor wanderer with shelter, when you see the naked, to clothe him, and not to turn away from your own flesh and blood?

Then your light will break forth like the dawn, and your healing will quickly appear; then your righteousness will go before you, and the glory of the Lord will be your rear guard.

Then you will call, and the Lord will answer; you will cry for help, and he will say:

Here am I.

If you do away with the yoke of oppression, with the pointing of finger and malicious talk, and if you spend yourselves on behalf of the hungry and satisfy the needs of the oppressed, then your light will rise in the darkness, and your night will become like the noonday.

The Lord will guide you always; he will satisfy your needs in a sunscorched land and will strengthen your frame. You will be like a wellwatered garden, like a spring whose waters never fail.

Your people will rebuild the ancient ruins and will raise up the ageold foundations; you will be called Repairer of Broken Walls, Restorer of Streets with Dwellings.

—Isaiah 58:6-12 (NIV)[21]

The natural step of allowing God to be part of our lives is that He begins to whisper and move our hearts towards the struggles of this world. He begins to nudge us in the direction of caring more for others than for ourselves.

For me it was becoming a part of the lives of these Afghan women and their children. When I did, yes, I encountered their sadness, but I also encountered their strength and their courage. Many times I felt helpless to change their situations. The institutions and the laws in Afghanistan do not exist for them.

Since Afghanistan is a visiting culture, women often get together over a cup of tea, and when they do, they talk. As I entered these women's homes, worked with them at the agency's office, or took care of them at the hospital, they shared their stories with me. Maybe because I was an outsider they felt able to verbalize their struggles, but I had also worked with some of them for years, and I had gained their trust.

What I began to realize was that my listening eased their burdens; they could share their stories with someone outside their society who wouldn't condemn them—and might affirm that a great injustice had been done.

I believe that is what Jesus wants us to do to those walking in captivity—walk alongside them, share in their pain, give them glimpses of hope, and work for their spiritual as well as physical freedom. Therefore, I share the below snippets of conversations and experiences so others may catch a glimpse and walk with them, too.

The sixteen-year-old girl jingled softly as she stepped toward me, balancing the tray of tea and snacks. She was the *aruse*, a new bride, still fully adorned with her golden bridal jewelry. She poured steaming hot tea into glass teacups and passed one to me. I thanked her, and welcomed her to our neighborhood. As we chatted, I inquired if she would finish her schooling. She hesitated, and diverted her eyes heavily painted with green eye shadow. Awkwardly, her new sister-in-law, not yet fourteen, giggled and said, "She can't go out, not until she has a baby." I was confused by this, was she pregnant already? Surely, they don't hide the women for the whole pregnancy.

Later, I talked with a long-term worker here in Central Asia who told me about a custom some families observed where the new bride is housebound until the first grandchild is produced. The bride is not trusted to be faithful, and this custom ensures the legitimacy of the child. As I thought of the twelve-foot mud walls surrounding her house, it reminded me of the fairy tale of Rapunzel, a princess who was locked up in her tower, awaiting her prince. In this society, she has married her prince…and his family has locked her away, and she would spend almost a full year housebound.

When the ancient bus shrieked to a stop, my co-workers and I boarded it and searched for an empty seat, pushing through the aisle full of children, sacks of produce, and flowing blue veils. We fell hard into our seats as the bus lurched forward. My co-worker stopped relating a story about her youngest daughter and fell silent. Scanning the bus, I noticed over thirty women on it, all completely veiled, wearing the *burka*, the blue fitted cloths draped over them concealing their faces, emotions, and identities. I was the only one dressed differently, though my head was covered, and I was wearing a long black coat that hit my ankles, I am considered immodestly dressed, and everyone could see my "naked" face. All the women around me stared through their prison walls of rectangular mesh screens. A hatred for the dehumanizing veil grew up within me. On the bus, because of the driver, an adult male, all women must hide their faces.

Walking with my head down through the swirling dust, I nearly bumped into a veiled form approaching us. The woman in the *burka* halted, pulled it back, resting it lightly on the top of her head. I realize there is a beautiful young woman beneath the cloth. She smiles at us. A friend with me extended her hand and kissed her on the cheek, "Azizem! So good to see you!" After we finished exchanging greetings, she slipped away. Then my American co-worker told me her story. She was a widow, not yet thirty; there was a man who desperately wanted to marry her. She loved him, but she wouldn't remarry.

"Why not?" I asked.

My friend explained, "She has three children; if she remarries she loses her children. The law says they belong to her husband's family. Currently, she lives with her in-laws, if she remarries, she leaves but the children stay."

The literacy class I was observing, packed with women, was deadly silent. The tears cascaded down the checks of the young girl as her body retched with sobs, and my eyes fell on her neck jagged with ugly scars. She had begun crying after another woman who had been mistreated shared. Her raspy voice blurted out, "My husband tried to choke me to death. A neighbor found us before he finished." With the back of her hand, she wiped the tears from her eyes;

"Where is he now?" someone asked.

"He is in Pakistan…free. I was exiled here, sent by my family to live with my grandma. What future do I have now? What hope? I cannot get a divorce, and if I did, no one would marry me, everyone thinks I must have deserved it. I am young, what future do I have?" Her sobs continued, and her words are the truth, not just words of bitterness. Society will always view her with suspicion, that somehow it must have been her fault that her marriage failed.

"Look at this photograph," said a woman my mother's age, as she thrust it in front of me. It was a black-and-white photograph of a young girl with short bobbed hair, wearing sixties'-styled clothing, and a young man in a suit. Smiling, they held a little boy on their laps, obviously proud parents. "This is how I used to dress. This was my husband, before he was killed fighting. Look at my hair! It is so free!" Tears sparkled in her eyes. That day her daughter was getting married, and I was a guest of the family. I glanced again at the plump woman in her fifties and the very conservative clothing she was wearing. If she did not have the faded photograph to show me, it is almost impossible to believe she dressed like that once.

"I was engaged to a man I loved. When my sister died, my family made me break my engagement and then marry her husband. I had no choice; her children needed me. It is what is expected." The young smartly dressed woman, a neighbor, who I was meeting for the first time, confessed to me as she served me nuts, raisins, and little chocolates on the side of a silver platter. She poured my tea, and stared at me, waiting for a response. I hesitated; I was unsure what she wanted—comfort, approval, shock. I couldn't imagine marrying someone, entering into such an intimate relationship because I had to. I gazed around the room: pink walls, golden-laced pink curtains, and pink pillows tossed upon the pink cushions where we sat. My stomach churned for it made me think of Pepto-Bismol.

"I have been married for fifteen year, but I still do not have any children. I have been to Kabul, to Pakistan, and no medicine has helped. They say it is my husband's problem. What do they do in your country for this?" The woman's searching and desperate eyes probed into mine, grasping for any hope. My heart went out to her because here if you have no children, you are nothing—no one in society, and you have nothing to do at home in this housebound culture. I marveled that her husband hadn't taken a second wife, since the wife, no matter what the doctor says, is usually blamed. This prompted my bold response. "You should marry another man. Take a second husband." For a moment, her troubles slipped away as she laughed heartily, and slapped me on the shoulder for my mischievous remark, knowing I had come to understand her culture, and the great pain both issues cause: second wives and infertility.

Glimpses of hope...

Arzu's face broke into a warm smile. She was a friend of mine, a woman in her mid-thirties. "Guess what," she whispered. "When I was in Mazar, I bought a *hijab*. The *burka*, the blue veil that I own is very old. I couldn't bear to buy another one. I am simply going to wear the *hijab* and a head-scarf."

"Just say you are from Tajikistan." I replied, grinning back at her, amazed at her courage. Only foreigners, teenage girls, and the Afghan woman who is head of human rights, walked around with "naked" faces in this remote city in the north. Arzu was throwing off her veil, and putting on a long black jacket, covering her head, and the lower half of her face, but to her it was a radical step. Her eyes would be seen, and for the first time she would clearly see.

This conversation reminded me when I had told her about Nicholas

Sarkozy, the former French president, who took a stand against the ultra-conservative veil that some Afghan and Pakistani women wear, and this created a lot of controversy in the media. "He made it illegal in France." I shared with her once over a cup of tea.

When I told Arzu this story, she paused and said, "Oh! I wish, if only we had a President like that!"

How old were you when you got married?" I asked.

"Age 14, 12, 13," the women's replies came one by one.

"I wasn't even wearing *tomboms*," the last and the eldest lady laughed as she pulled on her *tomboms*, the loose-fitting trousers worn by women under their long shirts for modesty. This indicated she had been so young, she had still been considered a child, free enough to roam and run in children's clothing. "I was 7 maybe 8," she continued. "My father traded me to pay for work that he needed done. We were eight children. I remember being taken to my new home on a donkey, I was so afraid I would fall off the donkey. When I got to the house, I was the servant for several years. Later, my husband would try to come and find me, and I would climb a tree, make faces at him and hide." Tears are welling up in her eyes as she recounts this. "I knew nothing," she said, and a silence fell over our group. It was too much for even some of my Afghan friends because all of them have daughters.

"What ages were your daughters when they got married?" is my next question to the group.

"Age 18, 20, 22, 17," come the replies.

I sigh, relieved. I know many of these women come from poor families; their answers for their daughters could have been identical to their own. However, these women and their husbands didn't let their own daughters follow in their footsteps.

I heard a knock at our metal gate. I cautiously opened it, and an ample-bodied woman cruised in at full speed, almost knocking me off my feet. "She did it. My daughter has been accepted into the law program." We embraced, sharing our joy. "You know she wants to become a judge to help women. They always have to go to male judges who care nothing for their situations. Unfortunately, she will have to live away from her family in Kabul for almost two years, but I will help her husband take care of her children." These words spilled from the lips of my language teacher, her pride evident.

My mind traveled to another story about a seven-year-old girl who desperately wanted to go to school forty years ago, but her father thought it unnecessary and wouldn't allow it. The little girl cried every day for two weeks, begging to have permission to attend school. Finally her father consented, saying that if she wore a *burka* back and forth to school, she could go. She related to me how she had hated it, a young child fully veiled, but she wore it so she could attend school. The same prideful woman embracing me that day, so excited for her daughter—this was her own story.

"How come you only live with your grandmother?" I asked, as the young, timid girl of fifteen with jet-black, braided hair filled my teacup.

"My mother trained to be a midwife, and she is assigned to work for five years in a remote part of the country. My father and my brothers and sisters went with her, but I am the oldest, and there is no school for me there. I want to be a journalist, so I stayed with my grandmother to study."

Her lips trembled at the last remark. I could tell she misses her family. I think of the many rural areas in Afghanistan where there is a high maternal and infant death rate due to the lack of trained healthcare workers. I admired this girl her future goals, as well as her mother and their sacrifice.

I finished giving a woman an injection who was visiting some relatives in our city, and needed some medical help.

She said, "You know the Taliban have begun entering our city. They have become many."

"Are they threatening the girls' schools and the women?" I asked, knowing this was a common first step.

"Yes, they don't want the women to leave their houses even to do the shopping, but the people of the city are not accepting this. They say, 'Women need to go to the bazaar, there are many things women need to buy. Girls need to go to school. They can help us better when they can read and write.' I have not stopped shopping nor have the other women."

"Yes, you are right, and the people of your city are right. Women need to go out." I agreed.

What kind of injustices does God want you to be a part of in this world? As you draw close to him, he will show you his heart. He will open up to you a world that is hurting and one he wants us to love and to work for change. However, to be able to make a difference we must learn to hear God's voice, by spending time with Him. One way to do this is over a cup of tea.

Chapter 19

The Art of Making Tea

Soaking in God's Presence

A young woman, her jet-black hair tied back with a shimmery headscarf, carried a tray filled with almonds, pistachios, dried raisins, and chocolates all twisted inside golden paper. She placed a delicate glass teacup down, and slowly filled it to the brim with a caramel-colored liquid. A whiff of cardamom drifted toward me, tantalizing my taste buds. My friend sat down and urged me to eat, and refilled my teacup the moment the smooth contents was gone. Our chatter that mid-Saturday afternoon was peppered with laughter and sharing of her dreams of becoming a doctor someday. Numerous cups of tea later found me saying my goodbyes, with promises of another visit.

The ceremony of drinking tea is central to any visit in an Afghan home. From the moment a person is ushered into the best room of the house, the kettle is placed on the gas range, and the water is brought to a rolling boil. Then the household's enormous thermos is pulled out, and no Afghan household exists without one. The thermos is filled with loose tea leaves, either black or green, sometimes cardamom pods are opened and the seed inside is crushed and thrown in the pot with the leaves, and then the hot boiling water is poured gradually into the thermos up to the lip. The top is screwed on, and next the tea must *dam makuna* or steep.

I learned how to make tea by emulating the preparation techniques of Afghan women. In the beginning, I hesitated to serve it, knowing it was inferior. Being proud of their own tea-making methods, they would always bring this to my attention. Tired of hearing about how inadequately I made a pot of tea, I tried harder to mimic exactly how they prepared it. The fresh cardamom taste was my favorite. So I would make it with cardamom pods, opened and crushed in a mortar and pestle seconds before the water had come to a boil. After repeatedly watching Afghan women in order to figure out how much tea was measured in, I discovered it wasn't only the amount of tea leaves used. Before I was able to master it, I had to learn that it was how long the tea leaves were left to soak in the water. The leaves must soak in the hot water because tea that hasn't been left to steep a sufficient amount of time is weak, pale, and flavorless.

Once a visitor complimented me on my tea, saying, "You know how to make tea like us!" Another time, she dropped in for a visit. In a rushed moment, I prepared her tea. As I went to pour it out into her glass, to my great embarrassment, only hot, colorless water with a hint of cardamom came out. I had forgotten the tea leaves! What a difference it made. We laughed. Then, I quickly whisked it away and made another pot, making sure to put the tea leaves in, and giving it time to sit in the pot.

Our relationship with God can be compared to making tea. Unless, we spend time soaking and steeping in the presence of God, our Christian lives remain weak and insipid. When I was young in my faith, a pastor introduced me to an exercise in meditation. I call it having morning tea with Jesus or perhaps, you are a coffee drinker (like me) or a soda drinker or a latte, frappuccino, or flavored water drinker. Whatever your particular beverage preference—the concept of having a drink with Jesus is the same.

After preparing your beverage, close your eyes and image you are sitting at a table with Jesus. Have your drink in front of you, and picture Jesus sitting across from you. Now start talking to Him out loud or in your head, or however you are comfortable. The most important thing is to be honest. I use the same words I would use talking to my best friend. I always let Jesus know when things are not going as planned. I let him know when I am extremely disappointed or hurt, and when something has happened that is incredibly wonderful.

Sometimes, I can do this for only a couple of minutes, and other times it grows longer. During this time, I can tell God about that new job, take a sip of my drink...then I can tell God how devastated I am that my grandmother just passed away...pause, and then I tell Him about my problems or frustrations at work, or I can share how physically tiring parenthood is, or how I don't know if my writing will ever go anywhere. Then I sit, drink and listen. Holding nothing back, I invite God to be a part of these issues, and invite him to show me the solution.

God usually doesn't audibly speak. But, I am reminded of truths I know, a particular story in the Bible or Psalm to read. Other times, I will get a sense that this prayer will be answered, or I get clarity on a decision I need to make. Most importantly, I am connecting with God, sitting and soaking lovingly in the presence of God's Holy Spirit.

Chapter 20

An Apricot Tree of Abundance
Living a Fruitful Life

Lush yellow-skinned fruit were stacked in mounds on the rickety wooden cart. The mangos, now at the height of their ripeness, oozed nectar-scented perfume into the scorched summer day. Two little boys, *bachas*, ran up to the cart and each purchased one of these heavenly fruits, and then took turns splitting them in two with the edge of a dull knife. Salivating from the fragrance, they ripped them apart with short, eager fingers, and their teeth grasped the large pit in the middle of the fruit and yanked it out. The skin was pulled open as they devoured the sunshine-colored flesh.

Fruit is a pride of Afghan society. Delectable grapes of every shape, size, and variety, blushing apricots, fuzzy peaches, firm apples, sweet-and-sour cherries, and football-shaped, bubble-gum flavored melons, appear in succession all summer long. They are grown and exported throughout the countryside to be feasted on in hungry abundance after the scarcity of such treasures in winter.

In a country that has been inhabited by agricultural farming tribes since the beginning of time, the topsoil has been stripped away by sweat and hopes for a better tomorrow. When flying over the country in an airplane, the waterless and scorched mountainous land stretches out from one mountain peak to another, making it seem impossible that even a thistle could thrive in such a barren landscape.

Yet, these same mountains drip with snow in the early spring when it cascades and trickles into rivulets, and soon culverts fill, feeding underwater springs that tumble into mightier streams. In areas such as Kunduz and near Kandahar, vast reservoirs of water bring life to the plains, yielding the succulent fruit featured at every guest table and celebration throughout the summertime—their season of abundance. The fruit brings wide smiles to the children, who so often survive on nothing but bread and tea, and it also hydrates the common laborer as he cuts pieces of watermelon into squares to eat as he toils under the blazing sun. It even graces the table of every wedding celebration, bringing promises of goodness and fertility to many newlyweds.

In the Bible, the metaphor of fruit is used in combination with the Holy Spirit. The Holy Spirit simply put, is the presence of God with us. When we welcome the Holy Spirit into our lives, the presence of God enters into our lives, and it produces all kinds of wondrous and lovely emotions that are vastly different from whom we were before. Our spirit becomes alive with the presence of God.

* * *

Crack! I ran to the veranda overlooking our courtyard. Malcolm and Emily raced to the windows after me. Squinting through the downpour, we were trying desperately to see the gigantic apricot tree that was growing in the middle of the courtyard.

I had loved this apricot tree throughout all the seasons. I had observed its gnarled branches and huge trunk slumbering in the wintertime, dreaming of donning a frock of snow-white blushing blossoms in the springtime. The tree would then shed it after a fortnight for avocado-hued tresses that provided shade from the sweltering sun for both my children and the many rambunctious neighborhood children, as they laughed, swung, and sped on the sidewalk with their scooters. In the summer, its leaves would sag under the weight of the pale-green apricots as they swelled to the sizes of giant golf balls. In the fall, its luscious apricots now harvested, the tree tired of its vibrant locks and extroverted life, would put on a mottled drab nightgown and slumber for a time under a blanket of white snow.

Sometimes, the neighbor children couldn't wait for the hard green skin of the apricots to turn to the color of a sunset. Shima, our fourteen-year-old neighbor girl, with an incredible imagination and a love for games, would climb up the ladder and precariously use a stick to knock a couple of the unripe fruit off for the children below. I would catch her at it and warn them that the apricot weren't ripe, and that every one of them would get stomachaches if they ate the green fruit.

That spring, though, contrary to the summer of drought and surviving from river water, it had rained almost every day. I felt like we lived in the tropics, and my friend, the apricot tree, looked nine months pregnant with triplets. Every single branch of the ancient tree was laden with too many clusters of maturing fruit. We had already lost a large branch from another storm. When I heard the crack during the storm, I feared the worst—that the over-abundant fruit would cause another branch to fall, or maybe even destroy the tree.

But, that night we later discovered it had lost only one more branch. Aziz was devastated it had lost so much fruit. On that one branch were probably one hundred apricots. I was so happy the roots of the tree ran deep, and my shade tree endured.

One month later, Aziz declared the fruit to be ripe, and we harvested them, Afghan style. He found a large straight, thick branch. Emily, Malcolm, and another co-worker and neighbor, Jenny, each held the corner of an old sheet stretched tight. Aziz first started with the lower branch, and hit it square and fast, and as a group we clumsily moved together as we attempted to catch as many apricots as we could in the taut sheet. The lush beauties rained down, and Aziz methodically moved from branch to branch smacking away. When the sheet was full, we filled plastic bags and bowls with our harvest. In the end, it proved too many for us to eat.

Aziz was given a wheelbarrow full to carry home. I carried several large bursting plastic bags to our surrounding neighbors. The apricot tree had produced a bounty for many to enjoy.

Like an apricot tree laden with plump, ripe goodness, we will overflow with the emotions of the Holy Spirit because…the true presence of God is amazingly beautiful, and has a life-changing effect on us. The Bible says, "The fruit of the spirit is love, joy, peace, patience, kindness, gentleness, and self-control."

When the Spirit of God moves in my life, I develop into the person that God intended me to be from the time he created me. Like the apricot tree, I move through seasons of usefulness and time of resting. I am able to show love where I never thought it would be possible. I understand joy, a deep and abiding joy, so I know that even when my trunks and limbs are being rattled by storms and downpour, my roots run deep in the hope of Christ. I am able to endure, broken perhaps, but not destroyed.

With the Spirit active in my life, I develop patience with those around me, understanding that good things come to those who endure, like waiting for an apricot fruit to move through all its different phases. Time develops something that is to be relished, and can produce a bumper crop to be shared.

When we connect with our life-giver, we become fruit-bearing trees for all those around us—nothing short of the miraculous, not unlike eating a lush sweet fruit on a sultry summer's day.

The Holy Spirit also helps us to be compassionate and to recognize when the law of religion has been misinterpreted and causes those in power to abuse others through religious authorities. Jesus recognized this in the Pharisees, as I learned about the Taliban in Afghanistan, former Afghan war lords and leaders still in power, and I recognized them for what they were: modern-day Pharisees.

The Pharisees were the religious tyrants when Jesus walked. They were the learned scholars who were in charge of enforcing judicial laws and representing a religious presence to the Jewish nation. They were not concerned with the heart and philosophy behind the law, nor the kindness of God, but with the outward appearance and the rigor of laws that brought them earthly power that they could hold over others.

In scripture, Jesus treated the Pharisees different than everyone else. To their faces and in front of crowds, he called them out on their behavior and humiliated them. The Bible is full of accounts where he challenged peoples' ideals about how a religious person should interact with those on the margins of society. With the Pharisees, he used severe words to reprimand them. He called them hypocrites, brood of vipers, blind guides, whitewashed tombs, and he warned them that they placed heavy burdens on others while they walked around without a care.

The following phrase is repeated over and over during Jesus' encounter with the Pharisees. I can almost hear a sigh accompanying this: *"I desire mercy, not sacrifice."*

Chapter 21

Land Cruisers and AK-47s

Mercy Not Sacrifice

One by one, the sleek Land Rovers with tinted windows sped into the parking lot, crunching to an immediate halt around our vehicle. My heart beat faster as armored guards swaggered out of them, with Kalashnikovs, the Russian-style automatic machine guns, strung over their broad shoulders. Car doors slammed behind them.

Sitting in the mid-morning sunshine, we waited for the twice-a-week flight from Faizabad to Kabul. We were dropping off guests that had been staying with us, and were picking up several returning co-workers. John got out of the Land Rover to inquire what was going on. I stayed put along with my three-year-old daughter, and her best friend, Elias.

After chatting with one of the armed guards, John discovered that Rabbani, the former President of Afghanistan from 1992 to 1996, was flying out that day. Rabbani first gained his popularity as part of the Afghan Soviet resistance movement, the *mujahidin*, in the 1970s. When the Soviets left Afghanistan in 1989, an absence of leadership occurred, and Rabbani and his supporters took over Kabul in 1992, and he became President. During his presidency, bullets soared in an all-out civil war, when those who had been allies against the Soviet Union started fighting one another for control of Kabul.[22] The warring factions destroyed the beloved capital city without a moment of hesitation, fighting each other to achieve ultimate power of the country.

Rabbani was President when the Taliban swooped in, replacing one unstable government with one that brought unrelenting rules, endless sorrow and silent weeping. Before the nation realized what they had welcomed in, some of them rejoiced that the Taliban had brought to a nation suffering from post-traumatic stress disorder what Rabbani could not—a cease of gunfire and quiet evenings where sleep again could be found.

At the time I saw Rabbani, he was an elderly man wearing a different cloak of allegiance. He was the current peace negotiator between the Afghan government and the Taliban. His hometown was in the province of Badakhshan, where we were now living. Briefly, it seemed my life and his would meet at this small airstrip at the edge of the world.

I leaned forward in my seat waiting for a chance to see this former president. A car door opened, and security guards with their loaded AK-47s flocked to his side. I watched not an anti-Soviet mujahidin fighter, but a dignified elderly man in a black turban with a meticulously groomed long white beard stride regally toward the airport lounge.

If I had been less intimidated by his stature, or his entourage of armed bodyguards, I would have queried him about his thoughts of peace. Did he think it was really possible for this divided nation to achieve peace? My courage failed because I could not walk through a group of about thirty guards holding automatic guns. So I only observed, my thoughts reverberating through the depths of my brain as Emily munched on cookies and Elias begged to be let outside to collect rocks.

Had I known Rabbani would soon be dead, perhaps I would have braved the rifle-toting guards. Probably not, but tragically on September 20, 2011, two weeks after our paths crossed at that dusty inconsequential airport, a suicide bomber, in the name of discussing peace, entered his home in Kabul. He greeted the seventy-one-year old before bringing him and his negotiating efforts to a violent end.[23]

Rabbani was killed days after trying to raise awareness and get support from religious leaders to issue a ban against the most controversial and destructive issue of modern-day *jihad*: suicide bombings. Karzi, the current Afghan president, bestowed upon him the title, "Martyr of Peace." and, where we lived, feelings ran high for Rabbani, since it was his *sar-zamin,* his homeland. Enormous billboards of his picture and black mourning cloths appeared all over the city, and the public mourned for days across the city.

Others were bold and spoke what was on their minds, from more than one person I heard, "It is good he is dead. He caused much pain in his lifetime, and the work he was doing was all a charade."

Whether this is true or not, it is true that the Afghan government is full of former *mujahidin,* war lords, and those Taliban sympathizers that committed abysmal crimes often in the name of God. Combining religious ideals with politics and power is a vile concoction.

* * *

We had traveled to Kabul from Faizabad several days later, and I was riding to the Kabul airport on my way to fly out for a vacation. One of the drivers, who had worked for more than twenty-five years with our aid agency, pointed to all the extensive apartment complexes and retail buildings that have arisen in Kabul over the last ten years. As we bumped along the ailing road that was riddled with potholes, he went into a rant about the rich and those working for the government who only lined their own and their family's pockets with aid money, while cheating the rest of the population. It was something we often heard, and as I looked at the elaborate apartment buildings and mansions built next to mud structures, I could only agree. Those people put in power had the opportunity to rebuild their nation; instead they chose to build up their own bank accounts and family wealth.

They are no different than the Pharisees, claiming to serve God in the letter and the law, but ignoring God's compassionate nature.

In my own life, I am careful to realize that my actions can easily reflect hardness and selfishness more than a merciful perspective. I am not a *mujahidin* fighter. I am not a Pharisee, nor am I Taliban, but I am part of a body of believers who worship Christ. Sometimes, those claiming to worship a Christian God have killed abortion doctors, protested at funerals of service men that are homosexual, and told those needing refuge from war-torn nations to stay at home. The Pharisees were strict and unjust, and Jesus let them know exactly what he thought of them.

Jesus stated:

"Woe to you, scribes and Pharisees, hypocrites! For you are like whitewashed tombs, which outwardly appear beautiful, but within are full of dead people's bones and all uncleanness. So you also outwardly appear righteous to others, but within you are full of hypocrisy and lawlessness."

—Matthew 23:27-28.

The longer I lived in Afghanistan, I found out that being a Christ-follower serving with a merciful heart can come with a high cost—and sometimes the cost is your life.

Chapter 22

Foreigners Are Buried There

A Life Lived for God

I can't believe they are raising children there! Don't they know it is dangerous and a war is going on in that country? These thoughts ran through my head as I sat across the supper table from an elderly American couple at a guesthouse in Dubai. As we chatted about their recent visit to Iraq to see their children and their four grandchildren, all I could think was, *Who would raise their children in Iraq?*

I was appalled that anyone would be working with their children in such a place like Iraq when a war was going on. Then I glanced down at my enormous belly. I was seven months pregnant and traveling alone back to America from Afghanistan with Malcolm, my almost-three-year-old son. John would join us in America in a month, when it was nearer to my due date.

Obviously! Then I realized for the first time *how others must have viewed me.*

To us, Afghanistan was a nation of tea drinkers and farmers—and some other people who liked to walk around with semi-automatic rifles. It was a complex country with many rules, but being polite and taking care of their visitors was rule number one. For us who lived far from the fighting, *it was not a place of war.* Every night's news highlighted an area of fighting between the Taliban and either the Afghan national army or foreign military, and it was not uncommon for armored tanks to pass us in the streets or have Black Hawk helicopters fly overhead; however, we did not feel like we were living in a nation at war. After living there for a while, Afghanistan even became "everyday-ish."

The dust and dirt, sporadic electricity, the burqa-clad women, the smell of frying French fries and grilling kabobs, and the heaping mound of melons lining the bazaar, had all become the expected. The helicopters and the occasional drone that flew overhead were our only reminders of the ongoing conflict in Afghanistan. I could never reconcile the word war with the sheep and goats grazing on the side of the hill, and the happy girls skipping to the school across from my house.

Yet, it was in the everydayness of life, that we encountered violent and brutal death of our national and international co-workers.

* * *

In the center of the city of Kabul, a small black sign with white lettering reads, "The British Cemetery." I never had the chance to visit it like I wanted to, but I know people buried there. In the local language it is called the *Kabre Gora*, the white man's cemetery. Two huge wooden doors in the middle of high mud walls are shut tightly. Go through these doors and the sounds of the city grow muffled and faint. Inside these walls lie the dead, soldiers of long ago.

This cemetery was created in the 19th century from the First and Second Anglo-Afghan wars, a time when the British were relentlessly trying to expand their kingdom. It is believed about a hundred-fifty-nine soldiers are buried in this cemetery from that time, although during those wars many more would have died, only ten headstones remain from that time.

Not only soldiers are buried there, but others who found themselves traveling through, living and being born, or dying in a place not of their own nationality. When they died, their bodies were placed here, often far from the place of their births.

The graves of thirty-some infants and children are found there along with approximately one hundred and fifteen other civilian graves. A long line of marble plagues can be found on some of the walls. The plaques list name after name of British service members who have died during the conflict after September 2001. Two plaques list the names of two dozen Americans who were killed in joint operations with the British.[24]

* * *

Thinking of these graves and this place reminded me of a front-page newspaper photograph that is forever pressed into my mind.

One of the mornings I was co-teaching at our preschool, I was sitting in a classroom, waiting for little rambunctious bodies to warm the preschool classroom up with their shouts and their calisthenics. Some well-meaning individual handed me a newspaper, stating, "Here, it is from England, it is only a week old, you might enjoy reading it." Usually, a newspaper written in English is a treat in a Persian-speaking world.

Immediately, the front page caught my eye. It was a photo of a young woman, maybe twenty-five, in a black dress with a red rose, as she stood weeping at the side of a tombstone. Reading the caption, I discovered her husband, a solider, had been shot and killed in Afghanistan. I took a sharp intake of breath, and then quickly put it away as the classroom filled with happy, smiling, singing Afghan, American, German, and British children.

After a week of thinking about that photo, I began to explore why it disturbed me so much and realized *it was not the Afghanistan I had known.* We had mainly lived in the north of the country, far from where the majority of fighting took place. I realized it was because the widow, who lost her husband in Afghanistan, probably had a completely different view of this land and people I had come to love.

I began to think about Shogufa, my co-preschool teacher and friend. I thought about our office manager, who works with John, that got married last year, and now he and his wife were expecting twins. I thought about the *chowkidor* who worked for us, and how he was a continual blessing and help. I thought about the little neighbor girls who came over to color and play with puzzles, and about the numerous Afghan houses that I had been welcomed into, drank tea in, and had laughed. I thought about the laughter of the neighbor children, sipping tea in a garden under an apricot tree, and being kissed in thanks on both cheeks by an elderly toothless woman whose face was covered in wrinkles. *This was the Afghanistan I knew.*

That photograph meant that some Afghan had killed this woman's husband, and a thousand miles away an individual grieved and had an image of Afghanistan that was contrary to my own. The world is a complicated place. I imagined for her the name Afghanistan could only bring her incredible pain and loss—and for me it brought smiles, hopes, and tears.

Even when death began to arrive on my doorstep.

Traditionally, humanitarian aid workers are the neutral parties in conflicts. The Geneva Convention is supposed to protect the well-meaning individuals who are there to aid humanity. Both sides are mandated to respect this in the understanding that if they needed aid or help, they will be treated as human beings, no matter what side they are on. We walked around unarmed and unprotected. The theory being we were not threats, and if we carried weapons, it showed we were different from the people around us, and carrying weapons actually made us more of a target.

More than once I would be walking down the street with blonde-haired Malcolm freely skipping in front of me, or we stood purchasing our ice cream or pack of gum from a roadside shop. A military convoy, armored tanks, heavy artillery, and soldiers dressed in bulletproof vests and helmets would pass slowly by, but we were not the ones that stood out. We didn't need weapons of war to be safe; we needed to know the local language and the culture.

Unfortunately, no one ever told the Taliban or the Armed Opposition Groups "the rules," or it was apparent that the lines had become blurred between humanitarian aid workers and Western Military. Therefore, they began to get caught or to be targeted like military convoys and journalists.

At first it was larger organizations that lost people like the Red Crescent (Red Cross in Muslim Nations) and the United Nations (UN). This was soon to change.

Death should not take us by surprise, but may we never grow accustomed to or accepting of brutal murder.

For us, working with relatively small humanitarian aid organizations, compared with the UN and the Red Crescent, it seemed to all start when aid workers pulled out of Kandahar because of instability. It was easily justified for Kandahar, a lot of concentrated fighting occurred there and it had always been more dangerous. We could still freely exist in and work in the rest of the country.

Then an American man who had worked there for years was kidnapped in a remote area of the country outside of Kabul province, where he helped set up hydropower electricity and infrastructure for villages. He was held captive for almost two months, and then rescued by the American Secret Forces. Two years later, he returned to Afghanistan to continue his work. In July, his co-worker and their driver were shot and killed outside of Kabul.

After that a young women who worked for an organization that had programs for the blind and handicap children of Afghanistan, was shot on the streets of Kabul—streets we often walked down. Buried in the British Cemetery, her gravestone reads, *"How lovely is your dwelling place, O Lord Almighty."*

Security began to get tighter, and we held our breath with the question foremost in our minds: "Who would be next?" Every time John's phone rang, my stomach tightened since one of his jobs as Regional Manager was security updates. Standard procedure was to use text messaging unless something major was happening, which required phone calls. But, the places and the areas that these incidents took place were fragmented, scattered, and usually remote.

Other people died in our community, causing us to grieve. An English teacher died of a heart attack and was buried in the British Cemetery. A twenty-two-year old woman, who brought beauty and who most people likened to a butterfly, died tragically of carbon monoxide poisoning. Today, a grape trellis grows at a girls' school in Maimana, a city in the north, dedicated as a gift to those she served and loved.

In the early spring of 2010, we had visitors in Badakhshan. A friend, who I had been in language school with, and her son, a photographer and a cinematographer, came to visit. She was there to teach a Birth and Life Saving Class to our community development workers, and her son was there to film the Afghan sports game, Buzkashi. We invited them over for dinner. Her son spoke of his plans to come for a year and do filming and media for different organizations. He wanted to highlight the positive changes and stories that were happening in Afghanistan. During his stay, he filmed an incredible video of a Buzkashi match in all its primitive power and force. He also spoke about a trip that might happen in August.

It had been a long time since any organization had done a medical, eye, and dental outreach in the remote Province of Nuristan, *the land of light,* and apparently one was being planned for that summer. If possible, he planned on going on this trip.

At the end of July, eleven individuals set out with permission papers in hand from the Nuristan Provincial government to run an eye-camp, dental clinic, and do emergency medical check-ups.

They would first stop at our office in Faizabad before heading to the province of Nuristan. The day before they were leaving, the vehicles arrived. The drivers slept overnight in one of our office compounds, and the rest of the team flew in the morning to begin the trip. In the morning I went over to set up some things for later that day. One of the drivers and watchmen for the group sat in the courtyard smoking cigarette after cigarette, as he waited to hear that the team had arrived at the local airport so they could begin their two-week trip. John, who was head of the Regional Office at that time, greeted the team and made sure they had everything they needed. The team then headed out towards Nuristan.

Two weeks later, the day before their planned return, Malcolm fell from a tree and broke his arm. We spent the afternoon at the German military hospital getting it x-rayed and set. The next day, Aziz, the *chowkidor*, knocked on our house door. Frantically he blurted out, "I heard on the radio. A group of foreigners have all been killed by the Pakistan border. Do you know if everyone is safe from the eye-camp group?" He was visibly upset and his body shook.

I quickly dismissed his concerns. "We had heard from the team several hours earlier, they should be here sometime this afternoon."

They never came.

Earlier that day, after crossing a stream and returning to their vehicles, they were ambushed and all were killed, except one of the group's drivers was spared. The next few days, the nightmare continued as all ten bodies were recovered and finally arrived in Kabul in body bags to be identified.

* * *

That first night I awoke in a cold sweat, and it marked the beginning of years of struggling with insomnia. The next day, I wrote the following in my journal:

They are dead! My mind grapples to comprehend the enormity of it all. I can't believe they have all been shot. The brutality of it churns my stomach, and a wave of unbelief washes over me again and again. The faces of the victims I knew flash before my eyes, and I try to imagine what they must have felt as they watched their companions being shot.

Ten people lay dead.

And who was the enemy—unarmed, aid workers. Did they know the effort that these workers made to reach these remote places to bring aid? Isn't it a right for people to have some basic health care in their lives?

I look at my son who had broken his arm this week, falling from a tree. He is very active, and this will set him back a bit, but he won't suffer the rest of his life because no one cared to fix it properly. He has lived in this country since he has been three months old. What does he know of Afghanistan? He knows that when guests come it is a great celebration, out comes the tea, the candies, cookies, and salty snacks. He knows about the snow-capped mountains that surround our city, he knows of sheep and the shepherds who on wooden flutes play haunting songs that float down from the mountains, he knows of discovering life with all his preschool Dari-speaking friends.

*   *   *

The impact of these aid workers' deaths was tremendous on us as a community. But, many who worked in Afghanistan stayed, for the same reason the people who were murdered chose to come to Afghanistan in the first place. Sometimes, God takes us on a journey, and that journey leads us to the unknown places.

When we are serving God, and our eyes are opened to the struggles that are happening in the world, and to what God cares about, it becomes impossible to be inactive. For those of us who follow in the footsteps of Christ, we devote our lives to love and serve the world, and sometimes this leads us into risky places from which we may never return.

Families of two of the aid workers chose to bury their loved ones in the British Cemetery. Etched in one of the tombstones are two Bible verse. One of them is from Colossians 3:13-14: *Bear with one another and, if anyone has a grievance against another, forgive each other; just as the Lord has forgiven you, so you must also forgive. Above all, clothe yourselves with love.*

Dr. Tom Little's gravestone has a stone cross etched into its surface, and simply says, *"You are so loved."* At the funeral of my friend whose photographer son died, they released doves in a symbol of peace and forgiveness.

Two years after the terrible incident, the father of another one of the victims who were killed came to Badakhshan on a trip to visit some of the places that had been part of his son's world. I imagine he was trying to understand and to make peace with what had happened to his son. He spoke of love and forgiveness as being the most important thing he wanted to express to those around him.

Were they all slayed as a result of a robbery? Or was it because they were foreigners, and they were killed that fateful day because of being from Western countries that were fighting in Afghanistan?

We will never know the answer to these questions. What we do know is that the victims' families, and those who knew them well, chose to demonstrate acts of forgiveness for what occurred. This demonstrates to me that they were acting out of a Biblical worldview. It is a natural emotion when we have been hurt to want to hurt back. But, this is not the way of the Kingdom of God. It is not the way of the taxi-driving shepherd, it is not the way of light, and it is not the way of love.

Dr. Tom Little, the director of the eye-camp, received the Presidential Medal of Freedom award for 2010 posthumously. The Medal of Freedom is the United States' highest civilian honor, presented to individuals who have made praiseworthy contributions to the security or national interests of the United States, to world peace or to cultural or other significant public or private endeavors. Other recipients that year were George H.W. Bush, Chancellor Angela Merkel, Dr. Maya Angelou, Warren Buffet, and Bill Russell, the former Boston Celtic's captain and Yo-Yo Mama.[25]

In President Obama's speech on February 15, 2011, as he addressed Libby Little, Tom's widow standing in his place, Obama quoted the verse from the Bible: *"Greater love has no one than this, than to lay down his life for his friends."* —John 15:13.[26]

Indeed, after all those years in Afghanistan, Tom Little and the others from the eye camp group did just this. The Afghan people were their dear friends, and their final journey into Nuristan was because of the love they had for the under-served and under-privileged.

And a life lived for God is one that is purposeful. It is a life that looks beyond my own needs and wants, and one that I give to God to go to the unknown places if that is where He leads me. A great injustice was done to the people I mentioned who died, but as Christians we live in hope that we will see them again, dancing, smiling, and fully alive. As believers we do not believe death is a final stop, but simply a pause, and we believe that one day Jesus will return and all will be restored.

> *"He will wipe away every tear from their eyes, and death shall be no more, neither shall there be mourning, nor crying, nor pain anymore, for the former things have passed away."*
> —Revelations 21:4

Chapter 23

Wedding Celebrations

An Invitation to the Marriage Feast of the Lamb

The music pulsated as I watched a young woman, lithe and controlled, enter the middle of the dance floor. She was wearing a flowing gown of gold and red, her raven hair was long and loose, and she began to move with the music as all the girls and women around her clapped in unison. The music from the keyboard rose to a crescendo, and her white stilettos shifted delicately back and forth as she twirled slowly and methodically to the pulse of the music.

All the women around me were smiling, engaged in the rhythm of the dance and moment of celebration. All of them were dressed elaborately; some of them wore extremely ornate necklaces of gold, gifts from their own wedding dowries.

The music stopped abruptly, signaling the end of the dance. The quiet seemed unnatural after the boisterous noise of the cranked-up speakers, but I welcomed the normal sounds of conversational tones after the deafening music.

Soon the music began again, and several children decided to give it a go. I thought of another wedding I had attended, and the dance of one of our particular young neighbor boys.

He pulsated and rocked to the tempo, imitating the traditional dance of Afghan men. He threw out move after move, until he was doing the classic shoulder pop, where one pops the shoulder back and forth with one's arms outstretched, dancing to the beat of the music. For the moment, everyone was captivated by this six-year-old star. I glanced over at the radiant face of his work-worn mother of five boys, and for a time her weariness was washed away, and she temporarily forgot the daily chores, delighting in the talent of her son.

* * *

Over my years in Afghanistan, I have been to a huge number of Afghan weddings. Someone in Afghanistan is always getting engaged or getting married, and often invitations come your way. The bottom line is Afghans know how to do weddings. Some of the most thriving businesses in Afghanistan are the expansive wedding halls that have been built in every major city. Although these weddings can often be a terrible financial burden to families, it is meant to be a blessing to everyone around them.

An Afghan wedding is no short ordeal. It is an all-day affair.

Sometimes, an elaborately written card, engraved in golden tones, will be delivered to announce the date, usually a couple days before the wedding begins—not months or a year before as we do in America. For men, the invitation is given at the office or a verbal invitation will be extended that day. For women, you might hear a knock on your door and a group of young female relatives of the bride or groom, dressed in modest prom-like attire, will enter your yard and personally invite you to come to the celebration.

Other times, jubilant music will float through the neighborhood, announcing that a wedding is happening. In smaller villages, if one of your neighbors is getting married, you are automatically invited and welcome to show up at the party.

Men and women celebrate separately. The men will gather at one place, either a wedding hall or a home, and the women will gather at another home or celebrate at the wedding hall after the men have finished their meal. Depending on how conservative the family is, sometimes the bride and groom will make an appearance together at the women's gathering, and sometimes they attend their parties separately. The men of the neighborhood come around mid-day when they are served an overflowing plate of *Qabili Palau,* the traditional dish of Afghanistan. The bride and groom are married in a small private ceremony attended by only the closest family members and performed by the *Mullah,* the Muslim cleric.

Wedding clothes are very important, and they happen to be the most counter-cultural attire I have ever experienced in Afghanistan. When you think of Afghan women, you often think of coverings from head to toe, and even when they look very smart and modern, there isn't an inch of skin showing, and their hair is neatly pulled back, and tucked under a headscarf.

For Afghan women, weddings are places to be free, and hair is unbraided, washed, and wore loose. The shinier your clothes, the more in fashion you are. Sequins, gold and silver, elaborate embroidery, tulle, and yards of bright fabric, crimson, lavender, chartreuse, and rose colors are all the rage.

Often, hands and feet carry new henna designs, or bright red or pink nail polish. Married women pluck their eyebrows, and the single women highlight their eyebrow lines. The more elaborate the better for eye shadow, the whiter foundation, and the brighter lipstick. Wrists, neck, and sometimes ankles are adorned with jewelry galore.

In wedding halls, shoes are kept on, in a culture where shoes are usually taken off in buildings. Amazingly, three-inch stilettos, with decorative designs and colors, appear to be appreciated by all.

Afghan men also pay a great amount of detail to their clothes for a wedding. They either wear three-piece suits with shiny shirts and black pointy shoes, or the traditional elaborately embroidered Afghan clothing. Cologne is slathered on and their hair is slicked back.

Dancing is also an important part of wedding culture, and they never believed me that I the foreigner cannot dance like they do. I don't even know how to dance very well in my own culture, and more than once my introverted self was dragged unwillingly onto the dance floor and commanded to dance. The horrible thing about this is the extreme confidence that Afghan woman possess when it comes to dancing, which means that usually only one or two people dance at a time so all the other women standing around can watch and clap.

I shudder even now thinking about the times I have made a fool of myself, trying to imitate their controlled and alluring movements. I have never been asked to dance twice at the same wedding; therefore, I can only conclude they finally believed me after I have given it one humiliating try.

The women usually dance until the food has finished cooking. *Qabili Palau* is a dish consisting of chunks of tender beef or lamb buried underneath basmati rice, with sautéed julienned carrots, plump raisins, and slivered almonds adorned on the top of each plate. When the food is ready, all the women eagerly sit on the floor, and long tablecloths are rolled out in anticipation of the feast. The children of the bride's family carry pitchers of water, soap, and towels around to each woman and so she can wash her hands. If it is at a wedding hall, the women sit at the decorated tables to enjoy their meal. Not only is each person given a heaping plate of *Pilau* to share with the person next to her, there is usually *Kofta*, spicy meatballs, and *Korma*, red beans and potatoes that have been slow-cooked to perfection, as well as salad and French fries. And then the banquet begins.

And you eat…and you eat some more…and you continue to eat. After you feel like your stomach is going to erupt, and if you take another bite it might all come back up—then the oranges, apples, bananas, and fresh fruit, which are always an expensive treat in Afghanistan, are passed out. This is followed by the *Firini*, a rose water or cardamom-flavored pudding that's sprinkled with crushed pistachios. And then the green or black tea is brought out, accompanied by sweets or chocolates.

What a feast! I have never eaten more than at an Afghan wedding, nor have I ever been served more extravagant meals. After I had been to several Afghan weddings, I began to understand why everyone enjoyed themselves so much. It is one of the only social gatherings where people literally let their hair down, dress flashy and showy in a culture where they are often forced to be subdued, and being a poor culture, a wedding isn't a time to hold back, it is a time to revel, and the dancing and food reflects this.

* * *

Hallelujah! For the Lord our God the Almighty reigns.
Let us rejoice and exult and give him the glory,
For the marriage of the Lamb has come, and his Bride has made
herself ready;
It was granted her to clothe herself with fine linen, bright and pure
for the fine linen is the righteous deeds of the saints. And the angel
said to me, "Write this:
Blessed are those who are invited to the marriage supper of the
Lamb."
　　　—Revelation 19:6-9

The wedding feast of the lamb is referred to in the last book of the Bible, Revelations. It is in context of the second coming of Christ, when Jesus Christ will come again and all things will be redeemed and made new. It is fitting that a wedding feast will usher in a new age: the time where all will be renewed, what was broken in the Garden of Eden will be restored, and there will be a final and forever victory over evil.

The new ruling of Christ will be ushered in with a grand party with an extensive guest list, and there will be eating and feasting and a grand celebration in Heaven—not unlike an Afghan wedding where it seems like every aunt, uncle, and cousin, as well as friends and neighbors are invited. A wedding is a direct contrast to how many Afghans live their daily lives. Most of them are forced to live with only the basic things of life, many of them have needlessly suffered the death of their own children due to lack of medical supplies and poor medical practice. Many have suffered senseless trauma as the result of the country's poor governance, the on-going terror acts, and almost every mother has a story about the loss of one of her sons due to fighting. During a wedding, it is a time to forget these pains, to dance in the moment, and revel.

Nothing will be more liberating than to be in God's presence forever, and all of the hurts and pain we experienced on earth will be forgotten as we live in the moments of pure freedom. It will be a time of tremendous joy, celebration, and a time of unity.

In an echo from the prophet Isaiah, we come to the end of God's ancient Biblical texts to us. It is fitting that it ends with an invitation.

> *The Spirit and the Bride say, "Come!" And let him who hears say, "Come!" Whoever is thirsty, let him come; and whoever wishes, let him take the free gift of the water of life.*
> —Revelation 22:17

It's going to be a mighty party. I hope to see you there.

Chapter 24

The Carpet Weaver's Masterpiece

Jesus the Master Weaver

Slipping my shoes off at the stone doorway, I entered the darkened alcove. The *pier mard*, the elderly man, with his white beard and devious twinkle in his eye, beckoned our group of foreigners to come deeper into the interior of his shop in Kabul. Standing in the very center of the dimly lit room, colors reverberated from floor to ceiling. The richly hued carpets—maroon, navy blue, ochre, walnut, mauve, crimson, and blood red—swirled together in a multitude of patterns that were neatly and symmetrically playing out in rectangle after rectangle of artistic endeavors.

Some of the carpets were neatly folded into squares and stacked on top of one another. Others were hung on the walls, intricately displayed in their entire splendor. And, still other carpets were folded over and in piles that leaned slightly, looking ready to topple at any moment, not unlike most of our precariously balanced lives.

The number of carpets in this shop was staggering, and I began to think of the thousands and thousands of knots that had been tied with nimble fingers and beating hearts. Each one, big or small, had a story behind it.

That day, we entered a carpet shop bordering Baba's Gardens, a famous garden newly renovated as part of the rebuild-Afghanistan efforts. I would have loved to dwell and look over each and every carpet. I soaked in all the colors and designs, and I was intrigued by the impact it had on me. Why the carpets carried such a sense of mystery eluded me. As I ran my hand over one, I thought of how the weaver ties knot after knot after knot to develop the detailed flowers, geometric shapes, and intricate designs. Each carpet seemed ready to speak, like it summoned the hungry onlooker to discover its story.

I didn't spend as much time in the store as I wanted. As the old man eagerly eyed us, I knew that if too many foreigners were together, we would receive the expatriate's triple price tag that came with having passports from other countries. If I looked at too many, engaged him in too many questions, my obligation to make a purchase would grow with each bit of information he gave me.

So we left the beautiful carpet shop, but I continued to reflect about them.

A traditional weaver sets up a loom, sometimes on the floor, sometimes upright. It is a simple mechanism usually made of wood, and is slightly larger than the size of the carpet it will weave. The loom is strung with undyed thread made of wool, cotton, or silk. The loom is strung top to bottom over and over again until the loom is full of vertical threads. When that is finished, the barebones of the carpet are now in place.

Then the mastery happens as the weaver begins to tie knots. One knot is tied onto a thread, and then the weaver moves quickly to the next string and ties another knot. Each knot will become part of the whole design.

Traditional weavers create designs into their carpets that have been handed down for generations. They may spontaneously weave the carpets with an order and a balance to their designs. The carpet is not meant only for feet to walk upon, but it is meant to tell a story and fulfill a significant purpose. Many carpets are given as dowries, and last the lifetime of the family. They in turn are handed down as heirlooms from generation to generation.

I bought a small carpet a few days earlier before our encounter with suicide bombers. It was my birthday, and we were looking for a carpet to go into the office I had set up for writing. The carpet seller, a personal friend of many people we knew, ran his hands over the carpet we wanted to buy, and told us how he buys his wool from a family in *Ghanzi*. He informed us they use the root of the wild madder, walnuts, pomegranates, and indigo to naturally dye their wool.

Natural dyes are chosen because of their ability to display color and change appearance in a variation of hues. In the carpet world dealers call this *abrash*. The carpets where the hues of color change in different lighting make the carpet more valuable. When the carpet we were looking at was placed in the sunlight, the colors shimmered and radiated deep earthen hues. Then I looked at it from another angle, and the colors darkened, giving a whole new appearance.

The carpet seller then told us the story of the design placed in the carpet. The pattern was a traditional bridal pattern of *se khima*, the three tents. A bride from the *Kuchi,* a nomadic tribe that continue to this day to pass their days in transitional housing, would create a rug that symbolized her migration from her old family to her new family. One tent represented her house, the other tent her groom's house, and the middle tent signified the joining of the families.

As enchanted as I was with my birthday gift, I was blissfully innocent of the fact that the carpet carried symbols that would play out in our own lives as we were about to become very transitional in just three days' time. Our journey of transitioning from living in Afghanistan for almost a decade to returning to our country of birth would suddenly be thrust upon us, and for a while we would be like the *Kuchi* tribe, migratory moving from place to place, packing and repacking our bags, wondering where we would sleep and where we would find a home.

Now my carpet sits on our living room floor in America, and as I look at it, I still feel like it wants to speak to me as its intricate designs and colors interplay to create not just something to tread upon, but that it holds some secret wisdom of old.

I cannot help but think my life is a reflection of a carpet, and from the very beginning the anonymous carpet weaver has been weaving it into a masterpiece. Even in my mother's womb, from a tiny egg united with an even smaller seed, my life began. So did yours. It multiplied and divided and held fast to a safe place to grow and develop into a fragile tiny human being. The beginning threads of my carpet were being woven at that time.

They were similar to many other threads being internally woven, and when I gulped air with my first breath, the first colored knot was tied. My introduction to my world, my culture, and my parents, began shaping me from that first breath.

The knots in my carpet reflect my world of air that floated off the Mississippi River, and was impregnated with the smell of fish and yeast from the brewery that I would smell on my way to dance class wearing a pink tutu as a young child. Early knots were tied reflecting my shyness and fear of water, and the laughter and joy of sharing my life with two sisters.

Knots were added later, and I have a bright memory of my mother visiting our kindergarten class and laying on the floor so all my classmates could listen to the heartbeat of the new baby who would soon enter our home. Before too much longer, Aunt Carol came over and sautéed us split hotdogs for supper, and brought the news that we had a new brother.

Along with the good memories, there were also dark memories tied into my carpet. Like when my parents yelled and my sisters and I fought. Those gloomy and foreboding knots were mixed with the brightness and the goodness of the complex swirled pattern that my carpet was becoming.

Knots of a different design began to be tied into my carpet as I sought to understand the world around me. I entered life in a small town where everyone knows about everyone, but it seems like no one takes the time to understand your heart. Periods of intense loneliness appeared in my carpet, when I desperately was seeking acceptance and praise from those around me. And, I began to hear whispers that *my life was not all that it should be.*

A bold primary line runs straight across my carpet. It indicates the point in my life when I discovered the God of the universe loved me, created me, and my life was not purposeless but purposeful. After that point, the swirls became less dramatic, the disquiet in my heart settled, and the patterns became intricate as I continued my journey as a child of God.

Since that time, many more designs have emerged. Learning what true friendship is, falling in love, getting married, stepping out and taking risks—like crossing an ocean to discover lives and dreams outside of the country of my birth. Around the births of my children, the knots appear messy and the design disorganized as John and I adjusted to sleepless nights, teething babies, and the general fogginess that parenthood can bring. Over time though the design became more orderly again and bright happy strands were woven in by the kiss from their dirty faces, the dancing of their chubby feet, the sweet smiles and the laughter that came when they gulped down the last dregs of my morning coffee.

Like each and every person on earth, my carpet is unique. So is yours. Throughout it all, the master carpet weaver has watched as I have handed him different colors to weave into my carpet through my choices. He has directed the design when I have allowed him to, when I have submitted myself to his guidance. With his guidance, his designs are more intricate and skillfully woven, and they are laced with hope.

Reflecting back when I was not listening to his voice and allowing him to direct my choices, the designs are dull and unimaginative, and at times, ugly and full of dissonance—like a dark force woven into my carpet, mingling in with the brightness of the good threads. During those times, I always knew…the Master Weaver did not abandon me, his creation.

The threads that God wove into my carpet during our time in Afghanistan were beautiful reflections of who He is. There are strands of learning how to speak another language, the joy of communicating and the miracle of being able to pronounce words that at first seem so strange, and designs woven in from the deep purpose that John and I felt a part of in the rebuilding Afghanistan efforts. The delight of discovering the historical richness of Afghanistan's past, and traveling the mountains roads that opened up into deep valley and ravines, and knowing that for centuries people have planted and harvested in these areas. The beauty of being welcomed into an Afghan home and kissed on the cheeks in the traditional Afghan greeting by a gracious hostess time and again shines through the carpet.

All of our experiences were not positive, like our encounter with suicide bombers. From that experience, and the loss of other expatriate and national workers from acts of terror, the strands in my carpet frayed, and I would need healing to make sense of all the pain.

Chapter 25

Wahid, My Angel Unaware

Jesus Our Comforter

Have you ever met an angel? I have. Mine lives on the corner of a street in Kabul. Wahid owns a shop that sells all kinds of goods imported from Dubai and the United Kingdom. He carries American Garden peanut butter, Nestle yogurt, frozen chicken, and mozzarella cheese for making pizza. I almost cried the day I found his shop right around the corner from my house, because although it was only the size of a large storeroom, it had everything I needed in one place.

After having lived in a small village for four years without a refrigerator, where preparing meals was a daily struggle, and getting "specialty" items was a constant challenge, finding this shop was as amazing as a five-star hotel on a gorgeous beach.

Emily and Malcolm loved going to the shop around the corner with me, and the shopkeeper Wahid always had smiles for them, treated them with kindness, and usually they left with an extra Kit Kat or a juice box as a gift from him. But, it was only after having frequented the shop for about eight months that I discovered he had been sent from heaven to help me.

It was a Friday in late March, and I watched my five-year-old daughter with her blue rain boots wearing a dress with pink and white swirly flowers adorned with a large turquoise satin bow tied in the back, her blonde hair had two little braids that swung as she skipped down the side of the road to the corner grocery store. We were having guests for dinner and needed to run quickly to get some tomatoes and green peppers for the fajitas I was making for Friday night dinner.

Perhaps, because I was in a hurry, or because the road was unusually quiet that late afternoon, or because she had guardian angels urging her on, my daughter skipped faster, and I let her run whereas I usually made her walk next to me for safety when we were on the street. She rounded the bend in the road, and I briskly trotted to keep up with her. We went up the stairs, entered the glass door of the store, greeted Wahid, and went straight to the produce section to find the vegetables we needed.

The produce was located in the back of the corner store. With Emily beside me, I told her to look at the juices and pick one. They were opposite the tomatoes. I turned, grabbed a couple of tomatoes and placed them on the weighing scale. I turned to get more, enough for half a kilo. Suddenly we heard the loudest noise ever, and in slow motion I saw thousands of pieces of flying shards of glass. With horror I realized it was a bomb! "It's finally happened," ran through my mind. My worst fear of being in the wrong place at the wrong time had come true.

Rapid gunfire began out on the street.

Turning to Emily I said, "Get down. Get down!" She began to cry. I noticed the produce department was the only place where the glass hadn't shattered. I crouched over Emily trying to protect her, and sobbed, "Jesus, Jesus, Jesus."

My mind rapidly began to process the situation, and fear rose within me. I was terrified the target of the car bomb was the store, and the Taliban were going to enter the store at any moment and find a foreign woman and child in the shop. I feared that we would be shot in a matter of seconds. The Taliban had already attacked stores, restaurants, and hotels in Kabul that were frequented by foreigners.

I pleaded with Emily, "You can't cry; we have to be quiet."

I feared she would be heard if they entered the store. I frantically began to look for a place to hide. Shelves in the store were knocked over, produce lay everywhere, all the windows in the rest of the store were all over the floor in zillions of fragments, the produce shelves were thin, and not deep enough for hiding under. I switched my plan: if we can't hide, maybe I can find a place to hide Emily.

I can die, but her life can't end this way, I thought.

I continued to scan the area. My mind raced in a frantic panic. I couldn't find any place safe for her, and the feeling of hopelessness engulfed me. I feared our lives would soon be over, and our images plastered across the evening news.

But thankfully it wasn't the guns of the Taliban that came next, but a familiar voice, saying, "Emily, Emily? I thought you left the store. Come, it isn't safe here."

I looked up to see Wahid, the storeowner, crouching over us. He picked up Emily, and his friend who often hung out at the store ushered us to the basement. Other young Afghan boys and men with fears in their eyes that matched my own were also hiding out behind randomly placed boxes. I went so quickly I forgot my purse.

As we ran, Wahid said, "If you and Emily had been out on the street a minute sooner. You wouldn't be here." I stared at him, unable to understand the enormity of his statement. I saw the adrenaline pumping through him as he quickly showed me the outer gates had been pulled down to stop anyone from entering the store.

I looked around at the shattered glass covering every inch of the basement which, besides the few boxes that the men and boys were huddled near, was way too empty for my comfort. I had never felt more exposed in my life. Every single half window was blasted out, and the metal grating that shielded the building was all that was left between us and the intense battle out in the street. The gunfire and heavy artillery exchange raged on.

"They are attacking the building across the street." Someone explained to me. I gulped. I knew people who lived there.

My phone rang. Though I had dropped my purse, my cell phone was in my pocket. The phone of the guy next to me rang. Everyone in that basement was on their phones. I quickly answered mine; it was John, trying to figure out where we were.

I knew we were not safe, but I was again powerless to make a decision. I had no idea where to go. Emily remained quiet as a stone. I explained to her then that a bomb had gone off, and we needed to stay. As we crouched behind a small stack of boxes, I began to devise a plan to bring other boxes around us so we could feel more enclosed. We were too close to the fighting in the street.

Then Wahid gave us more directions. "You can't stay here; it's not a good place."

I agreed wholeheartedly and followed him along with some others back upstairs through the store again. They had pulled back a section of the store shelf that was a secret door. It led to the apartments above. Before I entered, I saw my purse lying in the produce section. I ran and grabbed it in case the Taliban entered the store and found the purse of a foreign woman.

As we went up the flight of stairs, one of the men asked me, "Do you know Anna?"

"Yes, I do!" I had forgotten Anna, a another expat that lived in this building.

"Do you know which apartment is hers?" I didn't, but thought surely we could find it.

At the top of the stairs I saw Anna in the hallway with her door open, others were in the hall, a woman with some distressed children had blood running down the side of her face where glass must have cut her when the windows blasted out.

I had the presence of mind to ask, "Anna, can we come into your apartment until this is over?"

"Yes, of course!"

The shopkeeper put Emily down, and we entered Anna's place. All her windows and the front door to her patio were blown out. Because they had blast film on them, they had fallen in large sheaths instead of shattering into thousands of fragments like downstairs in the store. The whole apartment seemed exposed, and the gunfire and automatic weapons continued to interrupt our conversations and peppered our discussion.

"We can go in the bathroom," Anna said. "It is the only place where the window hasn't blasted out."

Emily, Anna and I went into her bathroom and locked the door. I finally felt a degree of safety. Looking down at my hands, I found I couldn't stop them from shaking. With the door shut some of the heavy artillery sound was muffled, but it still felt way too close.

"Let's pray," I said. Anna and I thanked God for this safe place, and asked for continued safety for the others in the apartment building, as well as for the place that was being attacked.

Wahid knocked on the door after a while. "Just checking on you." His friend came too, and with trembling hands as he inhaled deeply on a cigarette, he told us, "I want to move to a village, away from this city and all the fighting. But I worked as a translator for your government, and the villagers won't let me live there, so here I stay in the city where I cannot sleep." His English was perfect; it didn't surprise me that translation had been his former occupation.

Wahid bemoaned the cost of the damage to his building. He ran his hands through his hair, and said, "Don't worry, you'll be safe. We will protect you." He gestured towards the door where we could see that the other tenants in the apartment had grabbed their guns and were lined up in the hallway to protect themselves and the building from the Taliban.

"You know," he turned to me, shook his head and said again, "If you and Emily had been out on the street a minute earlier, you would have been dead."

"I know," was all I could reply.

"I will be back to check on you," he said as he left.

He came several more times giving us updates. The police forces had evacuated the building across the street where nineteen people that we knew, including several children, had been having an afternoon get together. The battle continued, with the attack focused on a small hotel across the street where people from other countries who were in Afghanistan on business or aid work stayed, and not on the original place I had thought.

"The Special Forces want to come up onto the roof of my building to fire against the Taliban across the street, but I told them I have people in here that need to be protected. If they come, the Taliban will start shooting at the building. You will be harmed," Wahid told us.

We sat for over three hours in that little bathroom. Waiting, at times making some jokes to try and lighten the dire situation we were in. Emily started to get hungry, and yet the gunfire and what sounded like grenades never let up. Anna's phone rang. "Anna, this is Bill. I'm with Special Forces. Tell me what apartment you are in, and who is with you because we are evacuating your building."

She told him, and three minutes later we heard a knock on the apartment door. We opened it and stared into the faces of men sporting full military gear. All I could think was, *We haven't been abandoned!*

We were escorted down the stairs, out the back entrance where we saw an entourage of military and rescue vehicles bumper to bumper along the whole street. The full force of the situation hit us. This was a major incident. We had a surreal moment as the Special Forces introduced us to the Afghan Special Forces who had secured the area and cleared the building we were in. "Do you want a picture?"

Seriously! I thought. *Am I going to post this on social media?* All I wanted was to get away. We stood for an awkward moment as they used Anna's phone to take a picture for us. Two English-speaking officers then escorted us to the nearby police station in heavily armed vehicles.

We entered the police station and were ushered into a room full of people monitoring and controlling the situation, and Afghan police and Special Forces services intermingled with British and American troops. A handsome and tall Afghan man in a three-piece suit began to question us as to why we were in the building.

In true Afghan style we were served tea, almonds, and candy as the military continued to monitor the situation. Emily quickly ate the candies. Suddenly, we heard a distant boom. One of the military men confirmed on the phone that another suicide bomber had blown himself up. A sick feeling spread through me because two bombers remained at large, and I thought of Malcolm and John a block away from where this was taking place.

We continued to sit there. We became a low priority for the Special Forces as they sought to deal with a real terror threat still at large. The local Afghan police milled around obviously not knowing what to do, since their headquarters had been invaded. Anna really wanted to go, so we began talking to them, and asking them if they could take us to a guesthouse run by our agency which was in the opposite direction of the fighting.

They were amazed at our language abilities, and as Afghans often are, they were very accommodating. They agreed wholeheartedly to take us where we wanted to go, and so we got permission and slipped out the door.

In a very surreal experience, we got in the back of the police truck and they drove off in the opposite direction of the conflict into the dark streets of Kabul. We passed juice stalls and roadside kabob shops that still remained open, even though not half a mile away two suicide bombers remained at large. I shook my head. People here didn't understand what normal should mean.

Soon we were at a familiar door, and as we rushed toward the gates, we were met with friendly faces. I would have to wait another hour before the last two suicide bombers had finally been taken out to be reunited with John and Malcolm. I have never been so happy to have my family together.

Our family left Kabul three days later. At that time we didn't know what it would mean. I didn't know if I could ever return. We went to Dubai, because we needed some distance to process things. Elections were coming in April, and we didn't know what that meant. This attack had been part of the Taliban's strategy to produce terror and to discourage voters. For the first time in my life, I truly understood terrorism, and what the Afghan people who get caught up in the terror attacks encounter. At this time, we had lived and worked in Afghanistan for almost nine years.

For the first two weeks in Dubai, a scene replayed over and over in my mind. The salty turquoise water lapping over my feet, the sand underneath my heels ebbing and flowing as the sea tried to drag it further out, the sun's rays warming my back—nothing could drown it out. I would close my eyes, and broken glass in millions of tiny fragments and shards would fly through the air, hurtling itself at me. A great terror would shudder through me over and over again as I turned and saw the frightened look of my five-year-old daughter Emily. It was a moment I will never forget; it was a moment of complete powerlessness.

And, though I sat by the beautiful Gulf sea, alive, a thousand miles away from that terrible experience, watching my laughing daughter wave-jump, I couldn't escape the memory of it. The beauty of the sea, the whispers of the waves, and the sunbathers who seemed to be having a red lobster skin competition, couldn't block it out.

But, then:

I would think about how God had Emily run faster that day on the street.

I would think about how though all the glass busted in the shop, we happened to be in the back of the store, which was the only place where the glass didn't break.

I thought about how God had provided a friend for us, and a safe place to be for the duration of the attack, and...

I would think of Wahid.

And, I know an angel that lives on the corner of a street in Kabul and owns a grocery store. His name is Wahid, and I'll never forget him. I know God sent him into our lives to help us that terrible day.

He owns a shop and sells all kinds of goods imported from Dubai and the United Kingdom. He carries American Garden peanut butter, Nestle yogurt, frozen chicken, and mozzarella cheese for making pizza.

Epilogue

My journey of walking in an ancient land—that had started when I descended the steps of an aircraft and stepped onto the runway of the Kabul International Airport almost a decade earlier—ended as suddenly as it had begun.

Our family's nine years in this beautiful country ended due to a terrible situation, but it is important that people know we loved this country. If you asked my children, Malcolm, now age twelve, and Emily, age nine, they'd tell you about the other children, visiting the neighbors, the food, and the other things they learned and will treasure the rest of their life. They still ask when we can go back. John and I feel the same—and if things were more stable, we'd go back in a flash.

After the attack we went to Dubai for a month, went through trauma counseling, and made the decision it was time to leave Afghanistan. First though we needed to say goodbye, we traveled back to Afghanistan so Malcolm and Emily could finish the last six weeks of school, and we could pack up our house and resign from our jobs.

Three days after we returned from our time in Dubai, three more foreigners were shot and killed, and another was shot and wounded in front of CURE international hospital. We had met them all. One of the doctors we had known for many years. It was too much; it was clear that the Afghanistan that we had known for all those years had changed.

In exactly one week, we were back at the airport. Our house had been hurriedly packed up, and we had purchased one-way tickets.

* * *

"Excuse me, Miss, I need to search your suitcase."

Lost in thought, I looked at the Afghan official and replied in Dari, "It's okay, go ahead."

He opened my bag and, surprised I knew so much of the local language, he asked, "How long have you worked in Afghanistan?"

"About nine years."

"When will you return?"

"I don't know," I paused. "I don't know."

"Well, I hope you do," he answered.

About the Author

Melissa R. Meyers has a B.A. in Cross-Cultural Communications from Bethany Global University in Bloomington, Minnesota. She has her Registered Nursing degree from Rochester Community and Technical College and a B.S.N. Completion degree from Viterbo University. She is a regular contributor for *Rochester Minnesota Moms Blog*. She has also published articles/stories for *Journal of Christian Nursing, Thrive Connection, Alive Now, Minnesota Conservation Volunteer,* and *Chicken Soup for the Soul* as well as other publications.

She now works as a neonatal nurse and enjoys spending time with her husband John, her two children, Malcolm and Emily, and their dog Jack. If she could she would live on coffee and chocolate. Most importantly she has a passion for others to know God and for them to live fully. If you would like to contact her, please email at: *BeneathTheAncientDust@gmail.com*.

Discussion Questions

Chapter 1: Traveling the Treacherous and Breathtaking Salang Pass

1. What stands out to you about the description of the journey on the Salang Pass?
2. Compared to the images that you have seen from Afghanistan, how is it different?
3. This chapter focuses on a journey, what kind of meaningful journeys or travels have you been on in your life?
4. Do you feel like you have ever been on a spiritual journey with God?

Chapter 2: Protective Walls of Rubble and Stone

1. What did you learn about Afghan society and walls?
2. What did you learn about the usage of walls in Biblical times?
3. The author shares about how sometimes we need to put up walls to get through difficult times. Do you think this is true?
4. What is important to process in this chapter, when we think of how we relate to others and to God?

Chapter 3: Turquoise and Gold: Discovering the Bactrian Hoard

1. Discuss your surprise about the extreme value of the lost treasure of Afghanistan.

2. Finding the treasure after years of war brought hope to the nation of Afghanistan. Have you ever experienced something good happening after difficult times?
3. Read Matthew 13:44-46. What do you think Jesus was trying to say in this parable?
4. Should this story mean anything to us today?
5. As the chapter unfolds, the author shares about how she "found God" as a child. Have you ever had a similar experience?

Chapter 4: Caves of Samangan

1. Do you enjoy visiting historic places? What kind of effect do they have on you?
2. What do you think about the author's question about how we as "finite beings connect with the infinite"? How do you try to connect with God?
3. Do you think we all have an innate sense that God exists?
4. Is it really true that God speaks through the everydayness of life?
5. Like the author did, when you look back at your life, can you think of experiences where you have heard the whisper of God?

Chapter 5: The Myth of the Mourning Doves

1. What did you learn about Afghan folklore?
2. Imagine a world prior to modern medicine. Try and describe it.
3. What stood out to you in this chapter?
4. Discuss some of the myths and superstitions that your parents or grandparents passed on to you.

Chapter 6: Tenacity—in the Hands of a Nation

1. Describe tenacity.
2. Read Luke 18:2-5. What do you think this parable is about?
3. The author thought that tenacity was a cultural value of Afghanistan; do you think this is true of your own culture?

4. What is Jesus really trying to say in Luke 18:1 about always praying and not losing heart?

5. What do you feel we can apply to our own lives from this parable?

Chapter 7: Donkeys and Demigods

1. Take a moment and watch some Buzkashi footage on YouTube. What do you think of the game?

2. Do you think it is true that we are look for a powerful hero to guide us?

3. What kind of king did Jesus end up being?

4. How does this make you feel about Jesus?

Chapter 8: Cucumber Sandwiches and Paintbrushes

1. Did anything surprise you about the story of Larissa's family?

2. Read Matthew 19:14, an often-quoted and discussed verse. What do you think Jesus is trying to say to his disciples?

3. If you have children or have experience with children tell some stories about how they grossed you out. Now share something they have done that delighted you.

4. What is something that you believed as a child that you no longer believe as an adult?

5. Is there anything else that stood out to you in this chapter?

Chapter 9: Meat for Eating and Ritual Sacrifice

1. Why do you think the author discusses Christianity, Judaism, and Islam in this section?

2. Read the story of Genesis 22:1-19 out loud as a group.

3. Was there anything new that you noted about this story?

4. How do you view sin?

5. Do you feel like forgiveness is really possible?

Chapter 10: Inmates Next Door, Morning Coffee, and Finding Freedom

1. Do you ever feel like your daily life is routine and monotonous?

2.   Can you do anything to change it?

3.   What do you think about the phrase, "God has a plan for your life?"

4.   How do you think God would describe your life?

Chapter 11: Tandoors and the Naan of Life

1.   Look at some pictures of Afghan *naan* found on the internet.

2.   Do you think we have a staple food in the West? If so what is it?

3.   Read John 6:35. What do you think Jesus was trying to say?

4.   Discuss similarities in food between the people of Jesus' time and Afghan culture.

5.   Why do you think Jesus uses food and thirst to describe himself?

Chapter 12: Our Taxi-driving Shepherd

1.   Look at images of sheep and shepherds from around the world.

2.   Read Psalm 23 out loud together in a new version that you haven't read before.

3.   Look at images of taxi drivers and taxis from around the world.

4.   What do you think about the author's comparison about Jesus being our taxi-driving shepherd?

5.   Jesus refers to himself as the Good Shepherd. What does this mean to you?

Chapter 13: Ancient Oil Lamps and Throngs of Cockroaches

1.   Read John 8:12. Does anything stand out to you in this verse?

2.   If it is night, or you are in a place without windows, shut off the lights for two to three minutes. Then light a candle, and discuss the difference a small amount of light makes.

3.   In Afghanistan, what are some light sources besides electricity that are used?

4.   Read Exodus 27:20-21. Why do you think God wanted a light outside the tent of meeting to burn all night long?

Chapter 14: Water in a Parched Land

1. Look at images of deserts. List all the ways you use water every day.
2. Where would you have to go to get water from, if it didn't come straight to your house?
3. Read the account of the Samaritan woman in John 4.
4. What stands out in her story ?
5. Have you ever felt spiritually parched or thirsty?

Chapter 15: Silverbells, Blackbells, and a No-named Rooster

1. Do you have any experience with chickens or roosters? Share your stories.
2. Read Luke 13:34. Then read the whole paragraph in which this verse is contained. Why does Jesus direct this statement at Jerusalem?
3. Do you view this verse differently after reading the author's story about being a chicken keeper?
4. How does this chapter and verse change how you view God?

Chapter 16: My Messy-Beautiful Worldwide Family

1. Describe your childhood family.
2. How is it similar or different than your current family?
3. Was this easy for you to do—or not? Why?
4. Are you actively involved in a religious community? If not, why not?
5. What are some steps you can take to connect with others?

Chapter 17: Befriending Bahar

1. Read and discuss some of the following Bible verses on poverty: Proverbs 31:8-9, Proverbs 14:31, Psalm 115:5-8, Psalm 146:5-9, Mark 10:21, 1 Timothy 6:17-18.
2. Finding lasting solutions to end poverty is a difficult task. Do you

think there are times when our helping others can do more harm than good?

3. Is it the responsibility of a Christian to help end poverty?
4. Is so, what responsible ways can you participate in helping to show Biblical love to those in need in your life and community?

Chapter 18: The Silent Whisper

1. After reading this chapter, did your perception of Afghan women change?
2. Which of the author's stories about Afghan women stood out to you the most?
3. Read Isaiah 58:6-12. How did this section make you feel about helping those in poverty?
4. If you have time, visit Afghan Women's Writing Project's website at *awwproject.org* to read poems and essays by Afghan women. Discuss some of these entries.
5. Do you think that Jesus challenged how women were viewed in society? If so, what are some examples that come to mind?

Chapter 19: The Art of Making Tea

1. What is one of your favorite go-to beverages?
2. Do you have meditation exercises that you have used before that made you feel connected to God? What are they?
3. What do you think of this method that the author describes in this chapter?
4. Schedule a time this week, to have a Morning Beverage with Jesus. Share your experiences.

Chapter 20: An Apricot Tree of Abundance

1. What is your personal understanding of the Holy Spirit? Your Church's viewpoint on the Holy Spirit?

2. Read Galatians 5:22-23. This is an often-quoted verse. After reading this chapter, does anything new stand out to you about the fruit of the Holy Spirit?

3. What season of life do you feel like you are in right now?

4. Take some time to find other verses about the Holy Spirit from the Bible. Share one or two in the group.

Chapter 21: Land Cruisers and AK-47s

1. Religion can sometimes be used to bully and make people obey. Can you think of some current examples of this?

2. Read Matthew 23:27-28

3. What were some of the names that Jesus called the religious leaders of the day?

4. Discuss the phrase, *mercy not sacrifice,* found in Matthew 9:13.

5. How can you apply mercy to people in your own life?

Chapter 22: Foreigners Are Buried There

1. In this chapter, the author discusses the dangers of working in a country like Afghanistan. Did your perceptions of Afghanistan change as you have read this book?

2. In your perspective, why do people go and work in dangerous places?

3. Do you agree that there are times when God will ask us to do difficult things?

4. What is your view of death?

5. Read Revelations 21:4, and share your reactions to this verse.

Chapter 23: Wedding Celebrations

1. What are some things about Afghan weddings that were a surprise to you?

2. What are some other Bible passages that mention weddings?

3. Read Revelations 19:6-9.

4. Why do you think the imagery of a bride and a wedding is used for the second coming of Christ?

5. Read 22:17 and discuss the invitation and what it means to you.

Chapter 24: The Carpet Weaver's Masterpiece

1. Take some time to look at Persian and Afghan carpets, or images of traditional carpet weaving.

2. The author describes her life as a carpet. If you were to describe your life as a carpet what would it look like?

3. What kind of story would it tell?

4. Would you describe God as a Master Weaver? Why or why not?

Chapter 25: Wahid My Angel Unaware

1. What was your reaction at the end of this chapter?

2. What did you think of Wahid? How did it make you feel about the Afghan people?

3. Do you have an example in your own life of someone that you felt God had sent at just the right moment?

4. Have you ever had moments where you have felt powerless?

5. How do you find hope in difficult circumstances?

Acknowledgments

Writing a book is a journey. This one in particular took almost four years to complete and get to the point of publication. I have so many people to thank. I especially want to thank John who encouraged me through this process. Not only did he live through many of these stories, he relived them when he was kind enough to read them as I was working on them. I want to thank Malcolm and Emily for putting up with their mom in front of the computer many evenings.

I also want to thank Kristy Wacek for reading a very rough draft of this book and helping me to realize that I needed to take it in a particular direction. I could not have done this without the help of Connie Anderson, book editor from Word & Deeds, Inc. Her ability to clarify and ask me to describe certain scenes was invaluable. I would like to thank Sue Stein for her cover design and formatting help.

Thank you Kate McCord for your friendship and heart over the years and your encouragement. I also would like to thank Mirjam Rheinlander, Cari Adams, Julie Jones, Kristin Krause, Samantha Bechtel, and Andrea Christenson for being proofreaders and giving your valuable opinions.

Last, I want to thank so many of the people I met and worked with in Afghanistan. So much of who I am today is a result of drinking tea with you, tramping through mud, living through tragedies, laughing with you, raising my children far from my homeland, and learning to speak in another language. Thank you.

Notes

Chapter 1

1. Nancy Hatch Depree, *A Historic Guide to Afghanistan*, Tokyo: Jagra. 1977, 113.

Chapter 3

2. Infoplease, "News and Events of 1978." Sandbox Networks Inc., January 26, 2017, *www.infoplease.com/year/1978.html*

3. Rachel Galvin, "The Golden Hoard." *Humanities*, November/December, 2004. *https://www.neh.gov/humanities/2004/ novemberdecember/feature/the-golden-hoard*

4. Andrew Lawyer. "Saving Afghan Treasures." *National Geographic*, December, 2004, 28-41.

5. Matthew Leeming. "Bactrian Gold, Bactrian Hoards." *Afghan Scene Magazine*, September, 2009, 23-25.

6. Andrew Lawyer. "Saving Afghan Treasures." *National Geographic*, December, 2004, 28-41.

7. Christina Lamb. "Lost and Found, the Rediscovery of the Bactrian Gold" *Afghan Scene Magazine*, September, 2009, 18-19.

8. *The New England Primer*, 1750 ed., p. 28.

Chapter 4

9. Nancy Hatch Depree, *A Historic Guide to Afghanistan*, Tokyo: Jagra. 1977, 374.

Chapter 5

10. C.N. Trueman, "The Medieval Church," *The History Learning Site*, January 2016, *www.historylearningsite.co.uk/medieval-england/the-medieval-church/*

Chapter 9

11. Surah 37: 101-107. *https://tsmufortruth.wordpress.com/2012/10/12/quranic-verses-ibrahims-test-of-the-sacrifice-of-ismail-stoning-the-satan-at-jamrat/*

12. Tracey Rich, "What is Rosh Hashanah?" *Judaism 101.* 2011. *http://www.jewfaq.org/holiday2.htm*

13. MJL Staff, "The Binding of Issac," *My Jewish Learning.* February 13, 2018, *https://www.myjewishlearning.com/article/the-binding-of-isaac/*

Chapter 11

14. Melissa Meyers, "Bread of Life," *Thrive Connection.* June 18, 2013.

Chapter 13

15. Victor Matthews, *Manners and Customs in the Bible; An Illustrated Guide to Daily Life in Bible Times*, Peabody: Massachusetts, 1988.

Chapter 14

16. John 4:9

17. John 4:10

18. John 4:11-12

19. John 4:13-14

20. John 4:15

Chapter 18

21. *Thinline Bible*, New International Version Copyright, Zondervan Corporation, 1996.

Chapter 21

22. Christina Lamb, "The Sewing Circles of Herat," *Perennial*: New York. 2002, 237.

23. *BBC*, "Afghan Peace Council Head Rabbani Killed in Attack," September 20, 2011.*http://www.bbc.com/news/world-south-asia-14985779*

Chapter 22

24. Andrew North, "Afghanistan's Graveyard of Foreigners." *BBC Magazine,* June 9, 2012. *http://www.bbc.com/news/magazine-18369101*

25. Office of the Press Secretary, "President Obama Names Presidential Medal of Freedom Recipients," November 17, 2010. *https://obamawhitehouse.archives.gov/the-press-office/2010/11/17/president-obama-names-presidential-medal-freedom-recipients*

26. *YouTube.* "Barrack Obama Presents 2010 Presidential Medal of Freedom Recipients," March 2, 2011. *https://www.youtube.com/watch?v=1uVYcAqMkPM*